STRIPPED

FROM RECOVERY TO LIBERATION

A Journey From Addiction And Prison
To A Life Of Faith And Purpose

JAMES ODELL

ACKNOWLEDGEMENTS

It has been a pleasure working on this book and I thank all of those who made it possible from the bottom of my heart. It was Brother Pat Burke who allowed me to share my testimony to a class full of inmates a few years ago. I became a testimonial speaker after he and his class inspired me and I went on to speak to thousands about the grace of God.

The relationship I have with my daughters and the love I have for them is a gift I want to express to them. A special thank you goes to Christian Life Fellowship Assembly of God Church, Jacob's Well Baptist Church, Bethel Treatment Center, Pearlington Christian Church, and First Assembly of God in Waveland, MS. I appreciate your support and love. Thank you also for allowing me to serve you and your community. You are in my prayers for exceeding, abundant blessings above and beyond everything you could possibly imagine, think, or ask for.

REVIEW PAGE

Thank you for purchasing my new book, "Stripped." Also please be sure to check out my other book called "The Road to Hancock County." Please take the time to leave a review on Amazon.com for this book. I truly appreciate your help in making this book a success. Thank you from the very bottom of my heart.

DEDICATION

This book is dedicated to Dan and Joan Munger. My life has been enriched by them, as have the lives of so many others. I am grateful to God for giving me the opportunity to spend the last five years of my life with them. It is from the depths of my heart that I express my gratitude to you for allowing God to love me back from an early grave through you. You believed in me during my darkest hour when I had given up on myself. Thank you and may God be with you.

This book is also dedicated to Sheriff Ricky Adam, Warden Zeringue, Captain Johnson, and all the brave men and women at the Hancock County Sheriff's Office. I will never forget you and thank you for the opportunity to serve you and your community for five years. My deepest wish is that God will continue to bless you and keep you safe throughout your life. It is with sincere gratitude that I thank you.

I would also like to express my sincere appreciation to Amanda. The help I have received from Amanda, an Atlanta public relations expert, is beyond my wildest dreams. She single-handedly made my first book a best-seller because she knows so much about the literary world.

CONTENTS

Acknowledgements..3

Review Page..4

Dedication...5

Chapter 1: It's Always Lonely at the Top 11

    Alcohol And Cocaine...13

    Straight To The Top...14

    Characteristics Of An Alcoholic......................................15

    Wanting And Wanting More 16

Chapter 2: Pride Comes Before the Fall.................................18

    Devalued, Frustration, And Disappointment.....................19

    Pride And Ego...20

    Overcoming Our Pride..22

    Biggest Lie In History...23

    Gospel, Faith, And Change..25

    Ignorance Is Dangerous..26

Chapter 3: Prison...29

    Self-Will Run Riot...30

    Matter Of The Heart...31

    The Right Perception..32

    Power Of Self-Deception...33

    Void In Our Hearts...34

    True Source Of Security..35

    Changing Our Perception...36

    What Matters Most..38

The Heart Don't Lie 39

A Startling Realization...40

Best Mistake I Ever Made 41

Faith And Humor 42

Chapter 4: Deny yourself..43

The Road To Hell 44

Mom, Hope, And Victory..45

True Repentance And Follower 45

Denying Christ Or Ourselves...48

Chapter 5: Humility..50

Rationalization and Justification.....................................51

The Root Of Trouble...52

The Right Decision..54

A Spiritual Malady..56

Desperate For Approval..58

Forgive Yourself 59

Life On God's Terms...61

Idol Of Self..62

The Way Of Humility 63

Chapter 6: God, Self, Or Satan.......................................65

Hold Every Thought Captive..67

Signs Of A Follower 69

The Only Solution...71

Believing Isn't Enough 72

Making Time For God..73

Spirit-Powered...77

Self-Induced Tortures Hell...78

Victor's Mentality About Scars...79

It's Not About Us..82

Greatest Feeling On Earth...83

Chapter 7: Humble Yourself...84

Fighting Sin Is Foolishness...85

Curse Of The Law...87

Understanding The Spiritual Malady.............................89

It's Who I am...91

Lived To Tell The Tale...92

Being The Change...93

Lukewarm Christians..94

Battle Belongs To The Lord..96

Chapter 8: Grace..99

How God Revealed Himself.. 101

Trust In The Lord.. 102

By The Grace Of God... 103

Count It All Joy.. 104

Your A Masterpiece... 106

Breathing And Believing.. 107

Divine Intervention And Hope.. 109

Instrument Of His Righteousness................................. 110

God's Power in Weakness... 111

Chapter 9: Stripped.. 114

Money Doesn't Solve Problems...................................... 115

False Comforters Aren't Comforters............................ 118

False Reality.. 119

Hanging By A Tether.. 119

It's All Perception.. 120

Seeking Something Beyond This World 122

Worthy Of Being Loved... 123

God's Unconditional Love... 123

Chapter 1

IT'S ALWAYS LONELY AT THE TOP

As with so many other nights in the ghetto, it was a sleepless one. It was a mother and her five-year-old son who were sound asleep next to each other. As she cried herself to sleep that night, she realized that her husband, the father of her eight children, was still missing. On that day, he went to work. However, it was also payday on Friday night.

She was sleeping on the floor when the sound of a slamming door woke her. The middle-aged woman woke up, looking at the clock, startled. It was 2:30 a.m., and the bars were all closed. It is obvious that she needs to prepare for what is about to happen. It happens at the same time every Friday night. All of the extra money her husband has is spent at a small town tavern called "The Creek" in the middle of the Dallas/Fort Worth metroplex. The town is named Arlington, Texas.

The hallway is filled with the sound of her husband shouting obscenities at her. Suddenly, the door crashes into the wall after he kicks it wide open. In response, my mother grabs me and pulls me closer to her. As if to protect me from what is about to happen, she wraps her hands around my head. As she pulls me close to her, she puts her hands over my ears. A lamp is slammed across the room by my father. As my father flipped the light switch in a fit of rage, the light came on. As soon as he sees me, his oldest son and first-born child, he stops dead in his tracks. After he walks out of the room, my mother begins to rub my face and tells me not to cry. Afterwards, she reassures me that I do not need to worry. There was nothing wrong with my father, he was just drunk.

I spent every Friday night that way for years. I grew up in a dysfunctional family where the only normality was abnormality. In my family, there were eight children. During my mother's lifetime, she was married twice. She had four children with each of her marriages. I noticed that my father initially drank a lot more than he used to, but that his drinking decreased over time. He would only drink one or two beers a week. I swore when I was ten years old that I would never treat my wife the way my father treated my mother. The other promise I made to myself was that I would be a better father to my children.

It was very difficult for my family to make ends meet. In addition to receiving food stamps, we were living in government assisted living. A month's worth of food stamps usually runs out about the last week of the month. It was common for my father and me to go down to the local grocery stores near where we lived and search for good food they threw away in their dumpsters. Since we didn't own a car, we had to depend on others for rides or walk everywhere.

My parents were wonderful people, but they both lacked education and worked minimum wage jobs. They were honest, hardworking individuals. They did everything in their power to raise their children to be honest. It is unfortunate that I made some very bad decisions when I was twelve years old. It was one of my worst decisions to begin consuming alcohol so young. In my family, there has been a long tradition of outlaws and moonshiners. As for the drinking, it dates back to my great, great grandfather. I come from a family of three generations of alcoholics. In my opinion, that is a reasonable assumption. The majority of those who passed away were affected by cirrhosis of the liver, which is caused by substance abuse. The worst thing I could have done to myself was to consume alcohol at such a young age. I consider this to be one of my worst mistakes. In retrospect, I wish I could tell that terribly troubled young man not to make that mistake. It would take me the next twenty-nine years to close doors opened by drinking at such an early age!

ALCOHOL AND COCAINE

The reality is that as you age, you don't get the chance to redo anything in life. Every person struggles with something in life. The very first month after consuming alcohol, I began stealing cars at night. I made friends with some much older guys who were between seventeen and nineteen years old. Their only commonality was that they were all intravenous drug addicts. Their habit was supplied by stealing cars, selling parts to mechanic shops and burglarizing houses to satisfy their addiction.

As a 12-year-old, I snorted my first line of Cocaine soon after my first drink. There was something appealing about Cocaine's effects. The problem was that I was afraid of drugs. It was King Alcohol's soothing effect on me that I found enjoyable. In response, I began drinking a few times a week when possible. After reflecting on my life, I realize that my drinking problem was ingrained from the beginning. Throughout my life, I have always consumed excessive amounts of alcohol. The majority of the time, I got drunk. I loved to be in the express lane on my way to the city of drunkville. As far back as I can remember, I rarely drank a few beers and then stopped. It would be impossible for me to stop at just a few. Even at twelve, I would drink ten to twenty beers every time.

My two older half-brothers also struggled with drug and alcohol addiction. Additionally, they became involved in criminal activity. A little over six months after I had my first drink. My so-called friends and I were arrested. All of them were sent to prison, while I was sent to a boys home in Burnett, Texas. I recited "The Sinner's Prayer of Repentance" shortly after we attended church on August 17, 1991. A couple of years later, I returned home, became sexually active at fourteen, and met the mother of my two oldest children. We were together for seven years, and I dropped out of high school after having my first daughter at seventeen. It was at this point that I began to consume large amounts of alcohol and developed the characteristics of an alcoholic.

STRAIGHT TO THE TOP

Around this time, my drinking began to become more problematic as a result of my high income. I was helping my brother's tear off roofs in the summer time for twenty dollars a day. Then one day my older brother's boss approached me about selling remodeling jobs for him. I accepted the offer of working off of commission only. With the promise of big paydays to come when I sold jobs for him. I did extremely well. I did better than my two brothers expected me to. I quickly went from making twenty dollars a day to making ten thousand dollars a month without ever getting my hands dirty. I had only one problem: my alcohol consumption had now reached epic proportions.

My actions would be those of any smart guy who wasn't taught how to deal with money responsibly. I lived beyond my means and was the epitome of financial irresponsibility. The list is endless: new cars, trucks, designer clothing, five-thousand-dollar leather couches, you name it, I had it! My sad reality was that no matter how much money I acquired, no matter what I possessed, I was never satisfied. There was always a sense that something was missing for me. I found it strange! Every time I ascended to the top of the roofing industry, got a new truck, moved into a bigger house, or married a better-looking woman. My first thought was, this is it! I remember thinking, this is what I've been waiting for! Nonetheless, it was bittersweet!

There was something horribly wrong with me. In my heart, I was empty. It is no secret that growing up poor gave me a fear of poverty. My fear drove me to the brink of insanity. Ultimately, my self-induced torment was an unimaginable torment caused by fear. In spite of the fact I wasn't aware of it at the time, I would soon discover two things that drive people. It's fear or faith!

It was at the age of nineteen that I began chasing hailstorms all over the midwest. In the beginning, I made approximately twenty-five to thirty thousand dollars per month. In my career, I became one of the country's top residential roofing sales representatives. In

1998, President Bill Clinton was in power, and by August, I was making more money than I could ever imagine.

I remember thinking one day, "This is crazy!" I watched my friends get murdered, overdose, and go to prison in the ghetto where I grew up four years ago. As a result of all this money, I am living a very comfortable life now. The moment I reached this point, I became very proud, arrogant, egoistical, and narcissistic. When I reached this point in my life, things started going from bad to worse. However, as long as there was a breath in my body, I knew and believed I was going to make money hand over fist, every day.

CHARACTERISTICS OF AN ALCOHOLIC

The inevitable happened and my wife gave birth to my second daughter. A few months later, I woke up one Sunday morning. As soon as I got outside of a convenience store, I cracked open a beer and enjoyed it. It was impossible to resist the temptation to have one more beer for dessert. That would be the second biggest mistake I ever made. The fact that I never managed to stop drinking, despite all my efforts, led me to abandon my family.

After that, I decided that my relationship with the mother of my two oldest daughters had come to an end. I fumbled in the closet, slid into my business clothes, and stepped over my two daughters. In the process of walking out the door. Then I turned around, taking one last look at my daughters. They looked like angels sleeping, but then something inside me said, "Don't do this, stay with your family." I opened the door and walked out because I needed another drink. The last time I saw my two oldest daughters was that fateful day. The last time we spoke was almost 23 years ago! My hatred of myself for making that mistake took me twenty-two out of twenty-three years to overcome. I literally almost drank myself to death because of that one mistake.

Over the next eight years, I chased hail storms and hurricanes all over the midwest and Florida. I would occasionally go back home to see my family. I went back home primarily to visit my parents. The main problem I had for those eight years was that I hated myself for walking out on my first wife and daughters after being with my first wife for so long. In a short period of time, we became dangerously codependent! As a greatly deceived young man, I was a sex addict, alcoholic, and suffering from a broken heart from what I had done to my family. There is still a deep pain inside of me that is indescribable. In my eyes, I had abandoned my family. Additionally, I believe that I was aware that I had become everything I didn't want to be.

In the era of my father's drunkenness, my relationship with my first wife was worse than that of my mother and father. I made my father seem like a priest, I was much worse than he ever was. It was as if I had made my father look like the perfect husband. In the event that you were to compare us. My mother and father remained together at least. I abandoned my wife and children and ran away. As far as I was concerned, I was a deserter of the worst kind. As a result, I drank myself half to death between ages twenty-one and twenty-nine. I felt this way the entire time. The annual salary I was earning was between $220,000 and $350,000. It would seem reasonable that I would be happy with that kind of money and opportunity. In spite of my best efforts, I was never truly happy.

WANTING AND WANTING MORE

When I walked into the Pensacola, Florida office of the company I worked for, the owner told me, "I see you have the most roofing jobs sold." I thought, this is it, this is all I need. It was natural for me to be at the top. As a result of so many sales representatives, this time was different. As the person who sold the most jobs, I lived at the summit of that mountain. Whatever accomplishments I made, the joy of them was fleeting no matter how great they were. It was impossible for me to pinpoint the reason why I felt like this at that time.

I remember watching television in a hotel room one day. A show called "American Greed" was on at the time. I was getting a divorce at the time from my second wife. When I looked over, I flicked my ashes into an ashtray and put my cigarette out. My eye caught sight of $120,000 cash sitting on a table out of the corner of my eye. Then I thought, "There's got to be more to life than this." What in the world is wrong? Why am I so blessed, but so unhappy? Despite having it all, I am the loneliest man alive! During my time in business, I have heard an old saying that stuck with me. Then something said to me "It is very lonely at the top." It became clear to me at that moment that it is very lonely at the top!

It has to do with the fact that I placed money before people. Therefore there was no one to share my life with or to even spend my money on. It was impossible for me to be satisfied with my security in money. This was due to my constant desire for more and more. The more I achieved at the top, the more I wanted. As a result, the top is no longer the top since it is always rising higher. Solomon was the richest and wisest person of his time. The Bible says this in the book of Ecclesiastes 2:24-26, "The best that people can do is eat, drink and enjoy their work. I saw that even this comes from God, because no one can eat or enjoy life without him. If people please God, God will give them wisdom, knowledge, and joy. But sinners will get only the work of gathering and storing wealth that they will have to give to the ones who please God. Thus, all their efforts are futile, like chasing the wind." I can describe my old life as chasing the wind. I had my stomach as my god, my destiny as destruction, and my glory was shame. The life I lived in my former life was absolutely horrible and I was never satisfied.

Chapter 2

PRIDE COMES BEFORE THE FALL

In the course of chasing hail storms and hurricanes throughout the United States, I drove and flew all over the nation. I traveled on and off for about eight years. A person's mental health can be destroyed by money and erroneous thinking. There was one thought process that I had on a daily basis that constantly ran through my mind. In my mind, I did not need anything else but money. Do you think that it's not proud of me that I felt I didn't need a relationship with God and that all I needed was money? That's amazing! My heart was deceived by Satan himself, the Great Deceiver. In my mind, money could buy me happiness.

However, that is true only to a certain extent. When you place your security in money, you run into problems. This line of thinking implies that Christ is not worthy of being our source of security when we do this. When we rely on money, people, places, or things to provide us with security. It devalues us when they leave. It is inevitable that people, places, and things will fail us at some point! As far as this thought process was concerned, because I got my security from money, when the money went away, or I didn't make enough, which is more like it, I was insecure.

In the same way that approval addicts seek approval constantly. When they no longer receive someone's approval, validation, or if that person moves or dies, they're devalued. The problem with that thought process is that it causes you to live a life of frustration and disappointment. It also robs the Creator of the universe of the glory in your life. Jesus Christ is the source of our security, and the basis of our self-worth. That is the way God intended us to think. We must be dependent upon God. In other words, our mentality should be that our job does pay us, but God is the source of our income. I might be very skilled at what I do to make a living, but I got my talent from God. We might have the favor of people, but God put that favor in the hearts of men to help us fulfill our God given destiny.

DEVALUED, FRUSTRATION, AND DISAPPOINTMENT

When a husband or wife is sweet and kind to us, God's love flows freely from them straight to us. As a result, we should believe that God is the source of the love we receive from our spouses and all the good gifts we receive come from Him. As part of a victor's mentality, you recognize God as the source of all your resources instead of people, places, and things he uses. It is true that humans have a significant role to play in loving one another. We must realize that Almighty God is Love, and in us, and He acts according to His will and good pleasure. That is exactly what the Bible teaches us.

The same thing happened when I was with my first wife. I had abandoned her and my two children. The love I felt for her was as deep as I could make it. Occasionally, I desperately wished for her approval. The lack of approval from her frustrated and disappointed me since her love was the source of my worth and security. In the end, I refused to forgive her for the things she did to me during our relationship. I became bitter, retaliated, and angry with her. Sadly, I started to build up hatred, violence, and murder in my heart towards her. This is known as the seven steps to bitterness. It all stems from unforgiveness. I wouldn't have been so self-destructive if I knew that God is the source of our security. I am trying to get you to think about how your heart is affected by the wrong mentality, just as it affected mine. In my opinion, it was proud of me to believe God forgave me for all my sins, but I cannot forgive my fellow man or my wife, the mother of our two children, for harming or offending me. This is a slap in the face to God, in my opinion. I used to be a very proud man in my previous life. After I walked out on her, I was angry that she wouldn't act the way I wanted her to.

The Bible says, "Love the Lord your God with all your heart and with all your soul and with all your mind and with all your strength. The second is this: 'Love your neighbor as yourself.'[b] There is no commandment greater than these." It is written, "Love carries no record of wrongs" (1 Corinthians 13:5, NIV, 2010). My point is that we must love others like God loves us and that is for who we are and where we are at, and not by what we do. In other words, unconditionally.

PRIDE AND EGO

When I was younger, I identified myself as a Christian. It's only been a few minutes since you finished reading the last chapter. In that chapter, my behavior is anything but Christlike. The point is that I said "I am Christian," but I denied it through my actions. I believed God had forgiven me of all my sins in my former life. My life was spent perpetually in sin. It was very proud of me to receive God's grace in vain, by living in perpetual sin!

Additionally, I would never forgive anyone for what they did to me in my past. There is nothing more proud than that, in my opinion. The Lord had forgiven me for all my sins, but I refused to forgive others. There's nothing more prideful or egotistical than. Especially since the Bible states, "Forgive or you will not be forgiven" (Matthew 6:14, NIV, 2010). There are numerous references to pride throughout the Bible. I would like to discuss the origins of pride in a particular scripture. The Bible says, "You told yourself, I will go up to heaven. I will put my throne above God's stars. I will sit on the mountain of the gods, on the slopes of the sacred mountain. I will go up above the tops of the clouds. I will be like God the Most High" (Isaiah 14: 13-14, NIV, 2010). Those are Satan's words that you just read.

Let's take a look at what happened in Heaven just before Almighty God cast Satan out? As pride is about self-exaltation, Satan had a great deal of pride. The basis of our pride is not only self-exaltation, but when Satan said "I will go up above the tops of the clouds. I will be like the Most High." Satan exalted himself beyond measure and implied to be god. We exalt ourselves above measure when we are full of pride, and say the same thing that Satan said: "I will be like God." Instead, perhaps we should say "I am god."

Allow me to explain what pride is and why it is the first abomination of God. It says in the Bible, "God is against the proud, but he gives his grace to the humble" (James 4:6, NIV, 2010). As well, Proverbs 3:34 mentions the same thing in its very last part. In the Bible, pride is taught to be the downfall of humanity, and it was born of Satan. Your choice will either be to serve God or to serve Satan. The kind of Father you have will determine whether you walk in light or darkness. Your choice is either to live a lie or to walk in the truth. Jesus said "I am the way, the truth, and the life no man will come to the Father but by me" (John 14:6, NIV, 2010). It is either your acceptance of Jesus Christ as the one-time ransom sacrifice and atonement for your sins that will bring you into right standing with God or your rejection of Jesus Christ will lead you to serve Satan's purposes.

This is all about pride. Don't you think it's proud of us to tell God that we don't believe in Him with our actions? Don't you think it's proud of us to tell God that we don't believe in Him with our actions? I will do you one better, if you say to God just as Adam and Eve did in the Garden of Eden. "You are my God, but you do not have the right to run my life. I will live how I want, but I believe in you." Your declaration is a way of telling Almighty God that you are a better god for your life. In effect, you are setting yourself up as the god of your life. If that isn't pride, I don't know what is. In other words, you are telling the Creator and Sustainer of everything in existence that he does not have the right to rule your life or to be its God. That is self-exaltation at its best and very prideful.

OVERCOMING OUR PRIDE

What can we do to overcome pride in our lives? It is only through humility that pride can be overcome. As soon as we accept Jesus Christ as our Lord and Savior. The way of humility leads us to overcome our pride. We do this as the Bible says, "If we confess with our mouth that Jesus Christ is Lord, and believe in our heart God raised him from the dead, then we are saved" (Romans 10:9, NIV, 2010). Don't let this slip from your mind! A person who is proud is one who exalts himself or herself and believes that he or she is better than other people. Therefore, we must clothe ourselves in Christ-like humility. Satan himself is the source of pride. You just read what Satan said in Isaiah 14:13. We must know this fundamental truth about pride and its origin, it is extremely important.

It's always Satan's goal to get you to do the opposite of what God would want you to do. It is important that you learn how the kingdom of darkness operates. I would like to compare God's kingdom to Satan's kingdom to illustrate my point. This will help you recognize God and Satan in humanity. It is God's kingdom that is a kingdom of light. There is a kingdom of darkness under the rule of Satan. The Bible says, "God is Love" (1 John 4:8, NIV, 2010). You are tempted by Satan to hate your fellow man, God's creation. There is an opposite to love, and it is hate. The truth is the way of God, and lies are the way of Satan.

In line with scripture, being the righteousness of God in Christ Jesus and living up to his righteous standard is the essence of God's kingdom. The kingdom of Satan revolves around living by the world's standards, because he knows you can't be both friends with the world and friends with God. The Bible says, "So, you are not loyal to God! You should know that loving the world is the same as hating God" (James 4:4, NIV, 2010). The kingdom of God is based on faith, while the kingdom of Satan is based on fear. The opposite of faith is fear. We are asked to walk humbly clothed in humility by God. It is Satan's kingdom's purpose to make us exalt ourselves above measure as he did before he fell out of Heaven.

The Bible says, "Those who exalt themselves will be humbled, and those who humble themselves will be exalted" (Luke 14:11, NIV, 2010). It is well known that Satan aims to destroy every aspect of your being and soul. Since Satan knows that Almighty God opposes the proud but gives grace to the humble, he wants you to be full of pride. The only way to receive God's grace is to clothe yourself in Christ-like humility and acknowledge God through his son, Jesus Christ, by confessing with your mouth that Jesus is Lord and believing in your heart that He rose from the dead. Do you think it is proud to say, "God I believe in you?" "However, you don't have the right to control my life." How about when people deny that God exists? That's a very proud thing for God's creation to say isn't it? In His love for us, God sent His only son to die on the cross. These are the ultimate acts of pride in our lives, causing us to exalt ourselves above measure constantly. As a result of these things, Satan can manifest himself through humanity.

BIGGEST LIE IN HISTORY

My purpose is to show you how Satan brought the spirit of pride to humanity. Our story begins with the fall of mankind in Genesis 3. I will explain how Satan, the Father of Lies works. He brought pride to humanity through Adam and Eve in the Garden of Eden. The Pentateuch (also known as the Torah)-the first five books of the Bible, including Genesis-is credited to Moses according to Jewish and Christian traditions. The Book of Genesis was written for the people of Israel, God's people.

The historical events have also been recorded for the benefit of believers throughout history (see 1 Corinthians 10:11). As the people of Israel wandered for forty years in the desert, Genesis was probably written there. It is likely that Genesis was written between 1446 and 1406 B.C., during Moses' forty years of leading Israel through the desert. A historical account of the beginning of all things is contained in this book. Additionally, the book records God's dealings with his chosen people. Today's Christians can know that they were created by God, who gives them their physical and spiritual beginnings, just as God's people of old did. Our significance and love are assured to us as his new creation. Just as God promised Israel, he has promised to give us a land to call our own, a wonderful land where we will dwell with him forever. My good friend, Heaven is our promised land.

Genesis refers to "beginnings," and its name gives us insight into its content and purpose. As we read the book, we learn about the beginning of the universe, the earth, the human race, and, perhaps most importantly, salvation begins here. The climax of creation was the creation of Adam and Eve on the final day. Essentially, they are a part of God's creation since they were created from dust (thus indicating their relationship to the created order) and breath of God (indicating their relationship to God).

Adam and Eve did not follow God, which was a great tragedy. They sinned against him, causing a break in their relationship with him. They were thrown out of the Garden of Eden, and a life of struggle and pain followed. God, though, graciously presented the hope of salvation right from the very start (Genesis 3:15). We are then shown a pattern of sin in Genesis, followed by God's judgment, which is softened by his grace. This is a brief overview of the Book of Genesis. Allow me to explain how Satan manifests himself through mankind. As he has since mankind fell.

As described in Genesis 3:1, Satan appeared to Eve as a snake. The snake said to the women, "Did God really say that you must not eat fruit from any tree in the garden?" (2) Then Eve said to Satan "We may eat fruit from the trees in the garden." (3) But God told us, "You must not eat fruit from the tree that is in the middle of the garden. You must not even touch it, or you will die." (4) But Satan said to the women, "You will not die. (5) God knows that if you eat the fruit from that tree, you will learn about good and evil and you will be like God!" (6) The woman saw that the tree was beautiful, that its fruit was good to eat, and that it would make her wise. So, she took some of its fruit and ate it. She also gave some of the fruit to her husband, and he ate it. (7) Then, it was as if their eyes were opened. They realized they were naked, so they sewed fig leaves together and made something to cover themselves. (8) Then they heard the Lord God walking in the garden during the cool part of the day, and the man and his wife hid from the Lord God among the trees in the garden. (9) But the Lord God called to the man and said "Where are you?" (10) The man answered, "I heard you walking in the garden, and I was afraid because I was naked, so I hid." (11) God asked, "Who told you that you were naked? Did you eat fruit from the tree from which I commanded you not to eat?" (12) The man said, "You gave this woman to me and she gave me fruit from the tree, so I ate it." (13) Then the Lord God said to the women, "How could you have done such a thing?" She answered, "The snake tricked me, so I ate the fruit" (Genesis 3: 1-13, NIV, 2010).

Wow, did you hear what Adam and Eve said to Almighty God about their actions. It amazes me how neither of them took responsibility for their actions before Almighty God. There was a lot of blame passed around between them and Satan. The story of Adam and Eve shows how they exalted themselves above measure. The Curse of the Law of Sin and Death was brought to mankind through Adam and Eve in Eden under the direct influence of Satan. Adam and Eve's sin and rebellion against God contributed to the destruction of human civilization and the destruction of its relationship with God.

GOSPEL, FAITH, AND CHANGE

My whole life has been a life of sin and rebellion against God. I told you previously that I had erred thinking, and that alcohol and drug abuse compounded many of my problems with thinking. As my sin problem finally beat me into submission after forty-one years, I realized how much I needed Jesus! In addition, I realized this after renewing my mind with the Word of God and getting transformed through having the mind of Christ. All of humanity's problems stem from Satan's game plan. There is a sin problem in all of us!

The process started at the beginning of time. When it comes to the Word of God, the "Great Deceiver" himself will always do one of two things. The first thing he will do is to get you to question the integrity of God's Word. The reason for this is because Satan knows that faith comes by hearing, and by hearing the Word of God (Romans 10:17, NIV, 2010). In addition, Satan knows if he can get you to question the integrity of God's Word. It is possible for him to rob you of your faith because the Bible says, "Faith is the substance of things hoped for, and evidence of things not yet seen" (Hebrews 11:1, NIV, 2010). Likewise, he can also steal your hope and cause you to turn away from Jesus spiritually. The only way to have true hope is to have faith. If you don't have faith in God through Jesus Christ, as a result, you are tossed about like a ship without a rudder at sea. It is impossible to have true hope without faith in Jesus, because faith is the substance of things hoped for.

The importance of faith is due to the fact that without faith in God you will only find hope in yourself, people, places, or things. The only hope you have is in God through Jesus Christ. If you put your trust anywhere else, you will be doomed both in this life and in the next. The reason why that is so important, is because the Bible says, "The righteous will live by faith" (Romans 1:17, NIV, 2010). It also says, "For we walk by faith, not by sight" (2 Corinthians 5:7, NIV, 2010). The important thing to understand here, is that seeing isn't believing for Christians. The reason God asks his children to walk by faith and not by sight is because we are spiritual beings. Our faith must be rooted in things that are contrary to what our eyes see. Our faith must be in what God's Word says about us and our situation. The scriptures say, "Call things that are not as though they are out of faith" (Romans 4:17, NIV, 2010).

IGNORANCE IS DANGEROUS

It is also Satan's goal to get you to possess a form of knowledge called ignorance. As a result of ignorance, we do not have access to the truth, in this case the Bible. In order to prevent you from reading the Bible, Satan will do everything in his power to prevent it. In addition, Satan has a good understanding of the Word of God. He knows "Faith comes by hearing and hearing the Word of God" (Romans 10:17,NIV, 2010). Likewise, Satan knows that if you lack faith, you cannot walk by faith, because you do not know what the word of God says about you or your situation. Another important thing to remember is what Jesus said "If anyone loves Me, he will keep My word; and My Father will love him, and We will come to him and make Our home with him" (John 14:15, NIV, 2010). It's important that you internalize this. How can you say you love God if you do not obey his commandments because you choose not to know them? How can you be a hearer and more importantly a doer of God's Word? If you don't know the word of God.

The people I used to listen to told me "What you don't know will not harm you." What they didn't tell me is that what I don't know can kill me and have me burning in Hell for all of eternity! Obviously, that statement is a lie, a half-truth. This way of thinking will lead us to settle for second best in life instead of God's best for us. I am certain that this is the case. It almost cost me my life because I was ignorant of God's Word. I was alive physically, but spiritually I was as dead as a man in the grave because I lacked the knowledge of the truth. As Satan tells Eve in Genesis 3:4-5, "You will not die. God knows that you will be like God if you eat the fruit from that tree, so if you do that, you will learn about good and evil." Through her ignorance and her reasoning process, Satan slaughtered Eve and humanity as a whole. As long as Christians are ignorant of God's Word, Satan will make them slaves to sin.

In Genesis 4, Satan ridiculed God and then told Eve, "You will be like God. "I explained earlier that Satan was kicked out of Heaven because of pride. In Isaiah 14:14, Satan himself said, "I will go above the clouds. "I will be like God Most High." Then after his fall from pride which is self-exaltation. Satan came to the Garden of Eden and manifested himself straight through Eve right into all of humanity. In the Garden of Eden, Adam and Eve gave in to the temptation of doubting God's care for them, and they thought they could get along better by being independent of God's direction (Genesis 2:15-17; 3:1-6). Their Creator had the right to direct them, but they rejected it. In effect, they were saying, "I will not submit!" They refused to acknowledge God's worth because of their pride. As gods in their own eyes, they sought security within themselves. My former life was like Adam and Eve's when I set myself up as my own god. I was exactly like Satan before he was cast out of heaven, I was full of pride. In the same way Adam and Eve fell, I also fell: "Pride will destroy a person; a proud attitude leads to ruin" (Proverbs 16:18, NIV, 2010). The fall from grace I took was caused by my pride. This is why I believe pride is God's first abomination!

As a matter of fact, our pride is what poses the greatest spiritual threat to us. My belief that this is the absolute truth is undeniable. The pride I exhibited in my former life led me to ruin, and I spent the last several years of my former life in a self-induced tortures Hell where I had little quality of life. The power of humility is what can put an end to pride and bring you back from the brink of spiritual death. As a result, God in you, acting according to His good pleasure, can love and help others through you. Our humility also allows God to magnify himself through us as we die to ourselves. In the Bible, God frequently refers to the ideal relationship between himself and humanity: "I will be your God and you will be my people" (Jeremiah 23:7;24:7;31:33; Hebrews 8:10, NIV, 2010). We must never forget! We have chosen the way of pride, but God calls us back to the way of humility constantly (Matthew 5:5). Since it is our pride that keeps us from seeking God, it is a gracious thing for God to undermine the basis of our pride. He wants us to come to repentance, and save our eternal souls. When a person directs love or praise to himself or others instead of to God, this is called pride. In order to avoid pride in our lives we must recognize who we are and who God is. We owe all glory, honor and praise to our Creator and Sustainer, God!

Chapter 3

PRISON

A felony conviction led to my first prison term in 2007. Looking back, I still have difficulty believing that I participated in my own demise voluntarily. In my naivety, I would never have dreamed that I would emerge as a violent, insolent member of the criminal underworld after I left the Texas Department of Corrections. In the year leading up to my prison sentence. The company I worked for had a multimillion dollar budget, and I earned $30,000 per month as its General Manager. As a result of the power of self-deception, I plunged to a level that was absolutely horrifying.

The maximum security unit where I was placed in West Texas was nicknamed "The Rocking Robertson Unit." When I got to prison, I had two choices. As a way to survive, I could join a gang and subscribe to the sick and self-destructiveness. The second option is to mind your business and sit in your rack when something goes down, thus allowing others to take advantage of you and robbing you of your dignity and respect. Therefore, I chose option one, harming myself and others as a result. In addition, it made me stay in prison longer since I was always in trouble. In retrospect, I should have served fourteen months and made parole. In spite of that, I got into so much trouble that I spent fifty-eight months in prison.

Today, I am no longer permitted to speak about the organization I used to be a part of, because I am now dedicated to doing the will of him who sent me and completing his mission. It was Jesus who said that, and today, through God's grace, I can serve the Lord faithfully. In retrospect, I realize that I had been imprisoned in my heart long before I ever entered a physical prison. I'm going to let you in on a little secret. In all, I've served time in seven different prisons, including two maximum-security institutions. However, my own private prison was the worst prison I've ever been in. That prison was built by me personally and my walls were so high around it you couldn't reach me even with a helicopter. It was my home for twenty-nine years. I was imprisoned by self-centeredness, selfishness, self-seeking, self-pity, self-righteousness, and pride in myself.

SELF-WILL RUN RIOT

I lived a life characterized by self-will run riot for many years in my former life! The Bible says, "Above all else, guard your heart, for everything you do flows from it" (Proverbs 4:23, NIV, 2010). In my former life, I spent forty-one years focusing entirely on myself. All I cared about in life was what I wanted and what I could get out of people. Every day of my life, I was trying to get rich or die trying. In all sincerity, I believed that I didn't need anyone or anything but money. At all costs, I would serve the god of money faithfully until my dying day. I saw money as the answer to everything in my life. That's how I lived for 29 years. As a result of that thought process, I became enslaved.

As a child, I grew up in poverty. I developed a fear of poverty as a result of that. There was nothing I hated more than going to bed hungry, walking everywhere, wearing hand me down clothes, or living in the hardships that a lack of money brought my family. The problem with serving the god of money is that it demands everything from you, at the expense of your soul! My arrest was the result of my thefts and con games with people and insurance companies. I have made a lot of money legally and I have also scammed quite a bit. There was no real intention to scam people, it was just a result of terrible thinking on my part. The lack of knowledge of Bible truth led to my dishonesty. The lack of knowledge of Bible truth led to my dishonesty. It was my philosophy that what they don't know won't hurt them. There was a problem with my definition of honesty. It occurred to me that if what I do benefits homeowners, my company, and myself, then it is a win-win situation. What is the problem with doing it? In that mentality, we set the standard for our lives instead of the Bible. This is also a slap in the face to God.

It was amazing how much money I made in such a short time. The irresponsibility and rebellious nature of my behavior basically ruined my life. It was really easy for me to make a lot of money. It was love at first taste! After I tried the good life, I was hooked! I determined my worth and value by how much money I made. My life would be miserable if I didn't earn what I thought I was worth. My value was diminished! As you can see, I was enslaved by money. There was never enough money, regardless of how much I made. In retrospect, that should have told me that something was terribly wrong with my heart and mind.

MATTER OF THE HEART

As far as this side of Heaven is concerned, there is one thing that is certain. The choice is ours to be slaves to sin or to righteousness. It would be wonderful to be able to go back in time and tell myself I was incredibly deceived as a young man, and why. One time, I heard a very rich and powerful man say that if you think you are better than others due to your wealth and materialism, then you are the poorest person in the world. During my former life, I was undoubtedly the poorest man on earth.

It is a sad fact of life that none of us get a do-over in life. We have the benefit of sharing our experience, strength, and hope with others, no matter how good or bad it is. In this way, we can heal, since we are only as sick as the secrets we maintain. When we submit to God's will, it also allows God to be glorified in and through us. As a result, we are making a living amends, helping others not to make the same mistakes. The Bible says, "For as he thinketh in his heart, so is he" (Proverbs 23:7, KJV, 2020). Another part of the scripture states, "O generation of vipers, how can ye, being evil, speak good things? For out of the abundance of the heart the mouth speaketh" (Matt. 12:34, KJV, 2020). When it comes to our hearts, the Lord weighs our motives. Ultimately, it all came down to the state of my heart when I was living in my previous life.

Sadly, my heart was laden with pride, arrogance, unforgiveness, bitterness, revenge, anger, hatred, and violence. Furthermore, I was incredibly selfish and self-centered. It never occurred to me that all these things in my heart would adversely affect the most important things in my life, relationships. My biggest discovery in life was that the most important things in life aren't things at all. In the end, it's about people and relationships. The most significant factor affecting my relationship with God was the condition of my heart. Sadly, pride was the main problem I faced. An individual who is proud is opposed by God, because pride is the exaltation of oneself. Basically, pride means that we think we are better than everyone else. I used to believe I was better than other people for numerous reasons in my former life. In my case, I felt cheated and unloved because I had been hurt.

THE RIGHT PERCEPTION

There was a story I heard one time about an individual riding in a taxi in New York City. There was a conversation between the man and the driver of the cab. Suddenly, a brand-new car pulled out in front of the taxi cab and cut him off. In heavy traffic, the taxi driver was stuck. In an instant, he looked to his left, swerved left, and hit the brakes. He narrowly avoided a serious accident. The driver who cut off the taxi cursed and shook his fist at him. There was no response from the taxi driver except to smile and wave at the other driver. In the back of the taxi cab, the guy couldn't believe how well the taxi driver handled the other driver that cut him off. When the guy in the back of the taxi said "Wow, that was really impressive. How did you maintain such a positive attitude during that?" The taxi driver then looked at the guy and said "Oh there is nothing to it. Most people are like garbage trucks, they just go around all day long dumping their garbage on others." The taxi driver said "I have learned after sixty years of life to keep my lid on my garbage can and not accept their garbage." That was a story I told because I used to be a garbage truck once upon a time. It was as if everything I had been feeling bubbled up to the surface like a spring. There was no end to the garbage in my heart that I poured out all over others. As my heart was sick and self-destructive, I bled it all out over the people around me, without caring who liked it, disliked it, or was hurt. In my world, everything would be customized for me. This was a perfect example of my former life.

POWER OF SELF-DECEPTION

In my former life, I was traumatized and acted as if I were a god. Through my actions, I told God just as Adam and Eve had done many years before me. "Yes, I believe in you, yet you cannot run my life." Pride is God's first abomination, because Satan is the father of pride and lies in Isaiah 14:13-14, which clearly defines these sins. It is amazing to me how prideful, selfish, and self-centered I was in my former life and didn't even realize it. A person's soul can be devastated by the power of self-deception. Fortunately, the living Word, which is Jesus, the Bible, and God's Holy Spirit of Truth, has now brought me the miracle of salvation and transformation. It is now possible for me to see my real issues, and to identify them with pinpoint accuracy, allowing me to provide help to others. It includes everything I'm going through now, as well as everything I've been through before. It gives me great joy to do that, because it allows me to help others avoid the same mistakes I made when I was younger.

I would like to state for the record, "It was said of King David, that "He shepherded them with integrity of heart; with skilful hands he led them" (Psalm 78:72, KJV, 2020). The heart of the matter is a matter of the heart!" In my former life, long before I became a true follower of Jesus Christ. I was conditioned to act and react in a certain way during my childhood. The truth is, everyone is accountable for their own actions, no matter what the circumstances may be. Furthermore, I learned that you are no longer a victim when you reach the age of eighteen, you are a volunteer! This is because we are old enough to know better after eighteen and the choice is ours to be ignorant of the truth. As adults, sin and rebelliousness against God are impermissible before God since we choose to ignore His infallible word.

Today, I understand how my heart came to be in such a terrible condition. It is all because money was the object of my hope, coupled with people, places, and things. In the past, I have trusted them many times but was eventually let down in one way or another. In my youthful innocence, I put my faith in people, not realizing that, regardless of their best efforts, people are human, and they will eventually fail you. Therefore, I was devalued, and I harbored unforgiveness, bitterness, retaliation, anger, hatred, and violence in my heart against those who let me down. The crazy thing was, some of them tried very hard to help me. The money I made or the help I received was never enough, and I was disappointed. I felt insecure and devalued when I didn't make enough money. In terms of putting my trust in places, I placed my trust in the company where I worked. Guess what, regardless of how many jobs I sold or how much work I did, there was no end to the never-ending cipher of never being enough. As a result of the false reality and sense of security I created, I felt constantly devalued and insecure. Throughout our lives, we must always remember that Christ is the source of our security, the foundation of our self-worth, and the only source of true hope.

VOID IN OUR HEARTS

We are all created with a God-shaped void in our hearts, and only Almighty God can fill that void with his love through his son Jesus Christ. In our hearts, this void acts as an internal compass guiding us to God, saying, "Fulfillment is what you're really seeking, from my love through Jesus Christ." In the Bible it says "But I, the Lord, look into a person's heart and test the mind. So, I can decide what each one deserves; I can give each one the right payment for what he does." "Like a bird hatching an egg it did not lay, so are the people who get rich by cheating. When their lives are half finished, they will lose their riches. At the end of their lives, it will be clear they were fools" (Jeremiah 17:10-11, NIV, 2010).

Let me explain something to you. My former life is summed up perfectly in those verses. I have learned a great deal over the course of my life. In my last moments, I would like to tell someone two things. The first thing would be to tell you that the Bible is completely accurate. Furthermore, I consider what God says to be absolute truth. It is essential that we live by fundamental biblical truths. This is the key to our eternity and the quality of our lives.

As King David once said "I have hidden your word in my heart, that I might not sin against you" (Psalms 119:11, NIV, 2010). My former life was so desperately filled with ignorance of God's Word that I almost died prematurely. I only had two life skills in my former life, outside of business: selfishness and self-centeredness! Looking back, my behavior was horrible. The good news is that I can now see it. I lived in perpetual sin in my former life due to my selfishness, and I hurt many people. Sadly, it was mostly people who loved and cared for me. A constant pattern of victimization was perpetrated against these people. The victimization of others and the victimization of ourselves are both consequences of perpetual sin. Our sin does this to us when left unchecked by Jesus. The consequences of this are very negative for our relationship with God and others. It profoundly impacts our psychological well-being and causes a spiritual imbalance within us.

TRUE SOURCE OF SECURITY

The relationship I have with God through his son Jesus Christ is something I am very thankful for. The fact that Jesus Christ is the source of our security and the basis of our self-worth should give us great comfort. As a matter of fact, the Bible says, "For we live by faith, not by sight" (2 Corinthians 5:7, NIV, 2010). It is written, "Consequently, faith comes from hearing the message, and the message is heard through the word about Christ" (Romans 10:17, NIV, 2010). It also says, "Faith is the substance of things hoped for and the evidence of things not yet seen" (Hebrews 11:1, NIV,

2010). The point is that without faith, one cannot please God. Our faith in God must be based on belief, and more importantly, we must trust God and his Word. In order to achieve this, we must study the Bible, receive his word into our hearts, and allow him to produce fruit in our lives through faith in him that is produced through the Bible, Jesus Christ, and the Holy Spirit. In order for us to accomplish this, we need to have faith in Jesus and allow Him to work in and through us.

In the Bible it says, "And we know that in all things God works for the good of those who love him, who have been called according to his purpose" (Romans 8:28, NIV, 2010). Hence, Almighty God is in control of our lives. It is God who has vindicated us and we can trust in him with our whole hearts. The moment we accept Jesus Christ as our Lord and Savior, we quickly realize that things are no longer happening to us anymore, but for us. He is the Creator of the Universe who breathed life into us and He is the Sovereign Lord who controls all things, everywhere, at all times. Essentially, God was saying in this verse that, despite our worst fears, even the worst things will work out for our good.

CHANGING OUR PERCEPTION

I would like you to consider this. The thought of being brutally murdered is my worst fear. The truth is that I know and believe "For we live by faith, not by sight. We are confident, I say, and would prefer to be away from the body and at home with the Lord. So we make it our goal to please him, whether we are at home in the body or away from it" (2 Corinthians 5:7-9, NIV, 2010). The Bible also says, "Precious in the sight of the LORD is the death of his faithful servants" (Psalms 116:15, NIV, 2010). In other words, when we live by faith in God our worst fears subside. Basically, what I'm trying to get you to do is change your perception from a biblical perspective. It's possible that you are experiencing a defeated, oh poor, pitiful me mentality. The Chinese philosopher Confucius once said, "If the goal seems unattainable, change the action steps." A Change in action steps requires a change in perception, since our thoughts determine our actions, emotions, and attitudes. The good thing is you can change your cognitive behavior through the Word of God and transform your life. We are liberated from our worst fears when we change our thinking in response to God's Word.

In truth, living by faith is living a life of victory. In the scriptures, it says, "So brothers and sisters, since God has shown us great mercy, I beg you to offer your lives as a living sacrifice to him. Your offering must be only for God and pleasing to him, which is the spiritual way for you to worship. (2)"Do not change yourselves to be like the people of this world, but be changed within by a new way of thinking. Then you will be able to decide what God wants for you and then you will know what is good, pleasing to him and what is perfect" (Romans 12:1-2, NIV, 2010). The Apostle Paul was saying that the word of God must transform us through the renewal of our hearts and minds. We come to a true repentance in this way.

Our minds are shaped by Christ in this way. As a result, we remain in faith and activate God's power in and through us, so that God can help us, and more importantly, through us, God can help others. What the Word of God says about you and your situation is important to know and believe. It is not enough to simply believe in God; even demons believe and are frightened. It is vital that we believe God's word. Therefore, the Word of God must be absorbed into your soul by means of your mind. Once it is written on the heart's tablet, you will never forget it. This will result in walking in victory rather than defeat, because you will have the mind of Christ and the words of God will be written on the tablets of your heart. God's Word will automatically govern your actions in your spirit, based on faith.

There is a very simple reason for this. According to scripture, "Faith comes by hearing, and by hearing the word of Christ" (Romans 10:17, NIV, 2010). In other words, the scriptures say, "The righteous must live by faith and walk by faith, not by sight." Through faith, God's power can freely flow to us, and through us, to help others. As a result, God is glorified in our lives. I would like to ask you a question. What do you believe? Do you walk by faith or do

37

you think like I used to? In other words, simply walking by sight, believing what the world tells you about yourself, your situation, rather than the Creator. Do you get tired of praying for victory and receiving defeat? Please allow me to make a strong suggestion. Do not underestimate the importance of your heart, it is one of the most important matters in your life. In order to achieve victory in your mind, I assure you that it must be infused into your heart by the living word, Jesus Christ, the written word, the Bible, and the power of the Holy Spirit.

As long as you live, keep this in mind. Our thoughts shape our emotions, attitudes, and actions, according to cognitive behavioral therapy. When was the last time you stopped to think about this? You were born with a reprobate mind; it is hostile towards God. Thus, it is extremely ungodly. As humans, we are naturally selfish and self-centered. The only way to counter that is by renewing your mind through God's Word. Through God's Word, you can transform ungodly thoughts, emotions, attitudes, and actions into Godly thoughts, emotions, attitudes, and actions. If we really research our lives, we'll discover that if we don't know God's word we're probably living a lie. In order to know God's final answer for humanity's problems, you must know God's word, which is the only way to know the truth.

WHAT MATTERS MOST

In your opinion, what matters most to God? How would you respond? I want you to pause and contemplate that for a while. I am certain that what is important to God is the purity and undefiled motives of your heart. It is important to take into consideration several factors when considering religion: what one does (actions, works, morals, ethics); how one feels (sincere, good, bad, indifferent); how one worships (ritual, liturgy, tradition); and how one appears in public. Scripturally, what defines true religion is the condition of one's heart. What are its characteristics? Is it open or closed, contrite or stubborn, soft or hard? "The sacrifice God wants is a broken spirit. God, you will not reject a heart that is broken and sorry for sin" (Psalms 51:17, NIV, 2010). The Bible says "My father taught me and said, "Hold on to my words with all your heart. Keep my commands and you will live" (Proverbs 4:4, NIV, 2010).

In the Bible, sin is any act, word, or thought that is not in accordance with God's will. King David said "How can a young person live a pure life? By obeying your word." (Psalms 119:9, NIV, 2010). "With all my heart I try to obey you. Don't let me break your commands" (Psalms 119:10, NIV, 2010). "Lord, I have hidden your word in my heart, so that I might not sin against thee" (Psalms 119:11, NIV, 2010). Ultimately, it is all about a person's heart! Can you tell me what the Bible means when it says "heart"? In the Old and New Testaments, the term "heart" appears 850 times in three Hebrew words and equivalent Greek terms. In 1 Samuel 25:37 and 2 Kings 9:24, they mention the physical organ that pumps blood in relation to paralysis or death when the heart stops). This is generally viewed as a metaphor for the spiritual organ within one's core self.

It is believed in biblical psychology that the heart is the innermost spring of life; it contains thoughts and plans, attitudes and desires, motives and choices, and is the seat of intelligence, emotions, and will. When my destiny was destruction, my god was my stomach, and my glory was in my shame! It was impossible for me to understand what was wrong with me. I never understood why, despite having it all by the world's standards, I was never satisfied. My appetite was always piqued for more and more. I felt like I was chasing a ghost! It took me a while to realize I was searching for something. It is now clear to me that I was searching for Jesus' love to fill the void in my heart that God uses as an internal compass to direct us to him.

THE HEART DON'T LIE

It was like my heart told me there was something more beneath the surface. Augustin called this a God-shaped vacuum, saying "Our hearts are restless until they find their rest in Thee." When I had reached the top of the roofing industry. That was fantastic, but it wasn't enough to fill my heart. I spent a decade partying.

Unfortunately, that only left me wanting more. My drug addiction almost led to an early death. In the process of trying multiple sex partners, I got addicted to sex. Our lives are short, and the pleasures we experience are fleeting. It was even my dream to be wealthy, so I bought new cars, trucks, condos, and tried to hang out with rich people. I thought, surely they know what life is all about. Sadly, most of the rich people I surrounded myself with were worse off internally than I was. My own experience proves that's a challenging task!

In the roofing industry between the ages of 18 and 29, I earned $2,200,000. It seems reasonable that a person with such an opportunity would be doing well internally. I was completely distracted from God's plan for my life by the money! My business performance was never a reflection of my internal performance. In spite of all the money, fine women, fine dining, and fine automobiles. My life was more empty than it had ever been before. It took me twenty-nine years to develop a sense of identity due to riches. Once I had done everything I could to get rich or die trying. There was nothing but selfishness and self-centeredness in my heart! In my mind, no one or nothing mattered to me. This included my wife, children, clients, and business partners. Let me ask you to read those last two lines again. My thoughts of God were no more important to me than my thoughts of the man on the moon. I had a sin problem that invaded my heart, hurt me and others, and it took a lot of courage to deal with it.

A STARTLING REALIZATION

I now realize that my relationship with God is what matters most in life. The reason for this is that I have the right motives in my heart. As I reflect on my life and creation, it is very clear to me that we should strive every day to give God the glory, honor, and praise He deserves. It is also important to remember that people are God's most prized creation. My former life ended leaving me without any relationships. The only things that interested me throughout my life were drinking, using drugs, having sex, and serving the god of money. An unresolved sin problem can take you to the depths of Hell. The best thing that has ever happened to me was meeting Jesus Christ.

As far as my former life is concerned, I mainly struggled with my God-given free will. I learned as a child that if you want something in life, you have to go after it. A man makes his own way, and the world never meets nobody halfway. My life was shaped by those half truths for 29 years. As a result of that thought process, I almost died young. It wasn't obvious to me at the time. My rebellion against God now seems obvious in retrospect. In my message to God, I said, "I believe in you, Lord, but you don't get to run my life." This is exactly what Adam and Eve did in the beginning. This was the message I was sending to God with my actions, "Lord, I accept all your benefits, including eternal life, long life, good health, and prosperity. I will not sacrifice my life for your sake."

In fact, I ought to have asked God to serve me instead. The idea that God was there to serve me really resonated with me! This was the most outrageous aspect of my heart and pride. As such, I was expressing in my thoughts, emotions, and actions "I am a fan of you Lord, but I will never follow you. I will never sacrifice anything I have in life to serve you God." Wow, I have a question for you. How many times have you spoken to God with your actions similar to that? You say "I love you to the Lord with your lips?" Yet, inside your heart, you have more gods jockeying for position than the city of Ephesus in biblical times? Do your actions say I love God, or do they say I would prefer to love and serve Satan the god of this world? How do you feel about yourself? What motivates you? Hopefully, you are serving God wholeheartedly out of faith. You may be experiencing some serious issues in your life. Let me make a strong recommendation. I urge you to take care of the matters of your heart before they destroy your life and possibly your eternity.

BEST MISTAKE I EVER MADE

As a forty-one-year-old man, I awoke half dead after consuming six shots of heroin a day in my former life. It was a life without joy, peace, contentment, or purpose. I felt like I wasted 41 years of my life. I lost everything I ever loved and cared about after making and wasting $2,200,000 dollars. This includes three wives, three children, and everything I ever bought with my money. Furthermore, I was arrested twenty-four times in four states and sent to prison three times in two states.

In that moment, I realized I had some pressing heart matters to settle, and I would die if I didn't. The punishment for sin is death. One of the best things that ever happened to me was God allowed me to be stripped of everything in life that did and didn't matter. The best mistake I ever made was being addicted to heroin. Consequently, I became aware of what is truly important in life. The most important thing in life is not a thing at all, but God's creation-people, and what our motivations are. This is what matters to Almighty God and should matter to us as well.

FAITH AND HUMOR

My first act of faith was surrendering my life to the Lord. My life has been filled with bad things, and I often wondered why they happened. Looking back on my life, I realize all the bad things I went through were like manure. Everything I experienced was meant to prepare me for my God-given destiny. The first time you put manure fertilizer in a flower bed, it stinks! It would be different if you returned a couple months later. There would be no smell, and there would be beautiful flowers all around.

In spite of the things that have happened in my life. In my mind, it helped grow me into the person I am meant to be. It is now clear to me that God, through all the setbacks and disappointments in my life, enabled me to grow, blossom, and flourish throughout all the bad and disappointing events in my life. God was trying to tell me that I need to grow from my experiences in life in order to stop repeating them. In order to achieve that, I had to address the matters of my heart. Every day, I give thanks to God that I am alive, that I have a purpose, and that I will fulfill my God-given destiny. My sincere hope is that your destiny will be fulfilled.

Chapter 4

DENY YOURSELF

A patrol officer escorted a middle-aged man from Texas into the Hancock County Jail on October 18, 2018. An officer strip searched the man and placed him in cell 131. He had a lengthy arrest record dating back to 1995. He was arrested for the twenty-fourth time in four states. The man wore a pair of designer blue jeans, red and white Puma shoes, and a black golf shirt. The great state of Mississippi charged him with four felonies. A variety of charges were brought against him, including drug and gun charges. My name is James O'Dell, and that man was me. As I lay in the cell, unsure of what was coming next, my world was about to change in a way I could never have imagined. There is no way that this script could have been written by the greatest Hollywood directors.

A few hours passed and I started withdrawing from heroin. I was never addicted to drugs until I was forty-one years old. I was addicted to heroin for seven months, before I got locked up. I was injecting twenty units of heroin, every three hours like clockwork, six times a day. It was so bad; I would wake up out of my sleep and inject heroin every three hours. It was a horrible addiction that became my god, and enslaved me like you could never imagine!

I had previously used cocaine, methamphetamine, ecstasy, marijuana, and LSD before heroin. The funny thing was that I was always scared of them. As a result, I stayed with King Alcohol. However, fate had other plans. As I was in jail in Ft Worth, Texas, my older brother owed me four thousand dollars he had stolen from me months earlier. When I confronted him about the theft, I couldn't believe what I saw. The girlfriend of my older brother was sitting there making him a fifty unit shot of black tar heroin.

As my brother was about to inject heroin into his veins, he stuck a needle in his arm. When my brother asked if I wanted any, I said, "no!" As a result, I went out drinking that night. My usual hangover greeted me the next morning. Once again, I drove over to my mother and father's house. Then my brother asked if I wanted a shot of heroin. As soon as I nodded, he injected four units of black tar heroin into my right arm. After a few minutes, it seemed as though everything was perfect! Unbeknown to me, I was about to experience a self-induced torturous hell that was unexplainable and unimaginable! There was no secret about my abhorrent and abject behavior. My ignorance of addiction, coupled with a lifetime spent making bad decisions, were about to lead to my early demise.

THE ROAD TO HELL

As I sat in the booking cell that night, I remembered the stories I had heard of people withdrawing from heroin. The events about to unfold would have never occurred in my wildest dreams. About four or six hours into withdrawals, I began vomiting uncontrollably. My mind began to race at a million miles per hour. Approximately ten to twelve hours later, my mind was racing, I had chronic diarrhea, and I was vomiting nonstop. In the process of using the bathroom, I would have to vomit as I was sitting on the toilet. An uncontrollable mess ensued. My goal would be to sleep as soon as possible. I had dreams about doing heroin as soon as I fell asleep. In the blink of an eye, I would almost get the needle into my arm, then I would wake up projectile vomiting! It was horrendous. This continued for about three days. As a result, I could not eat. The amount of water I could drink barely sufficed to keep me alive. Despite my best efforts, I knew I could not resist the withdrawal symptoms. On day three, when I had run out of strength to go to the toilet, I began urinating and defecating on myself. It was an absolute humiliation for me. It was always me who had all the answers. In this case, I was tired, sick, and tired of feeling sick and tired. As far as answers were concerned, I had none.

My thoughts quickly turned to suicide, and I quickly ruled that out because I did not want my children to remember me that way. I also knew that it would kill my parents, especially my mother! On day four, I lay there until the early morning hours. A semiconscious state overtook me as I lay there. The experience was as if I were dreaming. Although I was awake, I had a clear view of my wife and children, as well as some good and some bad times in my life. At this point, I prayed the most sincere and honest prayers I had ever prayed. My utter hopelessness and despair had reached a level few humans can possibly comprehend. I said, "God, just let me die."

MOM, HOPE, AND VICTORY

Afterwards, my mind continued to drift. As soon as I saw my mother, the strangest thing happened. As a child, I saw myself. The moment I boarded the church bus, my mother kissed me goodbye. The cross was then visible to me. My memory was jogged by God's existence. My memory suddenly flashed back to my church days when I was told there was hope and victory in Jesus. One preacher from Kingsland, Texas, stands out in my memory. A preacher by the name of Marshall Edwards delivered this sermon. When he preached, he would shout at top of his lungs, "THERE IS HOPE AND VICTORY IN JESUS!" It was as if he were right there with me in the cell. The moment I heard him say "There is hope and victory in Jesus," something inside me came alive again, because I remembered there was a God, and there was hope and victory in Jesus. During that moment, my entire existence rested on that hope. While I believed in God before, I had only surrendered a portion of myself to him in order to gain what I wanted from him. I fell asleep peacefully for the first time in a long time.

TRUE REPENTANCE AND FOLLOWER

The next morning, I awoke and began considering what had just happened. It was a long day for me as I was put back in the general population the next day and was placed in a cell with five to six

45

other inmates. It was impossible for me to sit up all the way for any length of time. In the first week, I lost 10 pounds. I took about thirty-five days to get back to normal after I stopped using heroin. Several weeks later, after reading the Bible almost every day, I bowed my head. In my prayer, I said, "Lord, I did it my way. I don't care what happens to me. I'd like to glorify, honor, and praise your name throughout my life." The fact that I had become the proudest man on Earth made it difficult for me to accept responsibility for my actions. That was not an easy thing.

When it came to living life on God's terms, it became apparent to me that I needed to learn how to do so. I would have to learn to die one day at a time to myself. The Bible says, "Whoever wants to be my disciple must deny themselves and take up their cross daily and follow me" (Luke 9:23, NIV, 2010). During my former life, I took the altar call at Buckner's Boys Ranch in Burnett, Texas at the age of twelve. I asked for the mansion in the sky, good health, prosperity, and to avoid hellfire. As I told you, I was willing to submit to God on my own terms, and in exchange for what He was able to do for me. The reasons why I wanted a relationship with God through Jesus Christ were all wrong.

It was my belief that Jesus Christ was the Son of God. However, I would deny in my actions that I loved him. According to the Bible, "If anyone would follow me, he must deny himself" (Luke 9:23, NIV, 2010). Though I tried to follow Christ, I never denied myself. It is clear from this verse that following Jesus is not possible with a casual arrangement and without any strings attached. A person can't follow Jesus without denying themselves. The phrase "deny himself" does more than just mean saying no to yourself - or even resisting yourself. There is no awareness or recognition of your own existence here. As Christians, we talk a lot about believing in Jesus, but we don't talk about denying ourselves much. This is a very unappealing message.

What can you do to deny yourself in a culture that emphasizes self-interest? We meet a man whose name we don't know in Matthew 19. As a result of his success, he is referred to by the

Gospels as the "Rich Young Ruler." My life was similar to that of this man. The man comes to Jesus with a question. According to verse 16, he asks, "Teacher, what good thing must I do to inherit eternal life?" That's a good question, and he asked it well. The question he wants to know is, "How do I get to heaven?" The way he asks it, however, shows that he only pays lip service to God. He asks, "What must I do?" That word means to earn or acquire. A good resume will get him in, he thinks.

He finally receives the message from Jesus about what he needs to do. Therefore, Jesus says "That if you sell your possessions and give to the poor, you will have treasures in heaven." Jesus invites the man to follow him, but first tells him to sell his possessions and give to the poor. As a result, he is forced to choose between following Jesus and keeping his stuff. A follower of Jesus could not follow him without denying himself. In spite of what many people have said, this story is more about following Jesus than it is about money. There is a crossroads at which Jesus places this man. A person can follow the money path or follow Christ; but neither path can be followed at the same time.

Taking all this into account, what does it all mean for you and me? Do you have to sell everything to follow Jesus? Yes, that may be true. It is more likely Jesus is saying these same words to you if you are more defensive about what Jesus said to this man. As this man in Matthew 19 describes, anyone who follows Jesus will come to the same crossroads. It is my pleasure to assure you of this one thing. It will take you stepping away from a different path before you can follow Jesus. Despite his desire to follow Jesus, he chose to follow his stuff over Jesus. It wasn't in his nature to deny himself. Are you ready to make a decision? My former life was marked by a choice not to deny myself, which nearly led to my death. There is a choice I have to make today. I can deny myself, die to myself, or deny Christ and die in my sin. If you reject Christ, may God have mercy on you, and please listen to me, the choice is yours.

When I was near the end of my former life. My life was similar to that of the "Rich Young Ruler" in Matthew 19:16-22. You can rest assured that it wasn't because we were both wealthy. It had to do with our mentality towards wealth. Our idolatry of money kept us from giving up our stuff for a relationship with Christ. It had never occurred to me, in my former life, to deny myself one time. I would go after another lady if I was married and liked her. It didn't matter to me if a hail storm was a thousand miles away, even if I would not see my family for months. In order to reach my career goals, I have sacrificed my family over the years. My money was more important to me than my family, friends, and even Jesus. My marriage did not prevent me from having sex outside of it. There was one thing, however, that I denied myself. A relationship with God through his son Jesus Christ.

DENYING CHRIST OR OURSELVES

This should be the only thing that matters in my life and yours. It is this startling realization that I finally come to at the end of the day. I have given myself everything I desired, and I have never denied myself anything. My biggest sin in life was denying myself the most important thing in life, Jesus Christ. My life had been a constant "yes" to myself, because I was desperately seeking the love of Christ. As a result of my foolish actions and ignorance of God's words, I had denied Christ. As I searched for the love of God in Christ Jesus, I lived in eternal ignorance of the fact.

In other words, I was always full of pride, continuously exalting myself above measure because I never denied myself anything. As a result, I was denying that I loved God enough to surrender my life to him through Jesus Christ. That is sheer foolishness, my friend! It is unfortunate that I hurt a lot of innocent people by my sick and self-destructive behaviors, and they were generally those who loved and cared about me. This is who paid the price for my own demise, as I led the charge! In light of these circumstances, I hope you have a clear understanding of how Satan, the "Great Deceiver," will take advantage of your power of choice and use it against you by trying to entice you not to deny yourself, exalt yourself above measure with foolish pride, and distract you from God's will for your life by using your power of choice against you.

As far as my former life was concerned, I overindulged in everything I did. It turned out that most of the things I overindulged in didn't matter. In my life, I rarely indulged in what really mattered. That's a relationship with God through Jesus Christ. Ultimately, it was my pride, foolishness, and ignorance that almost caused me to die prematurely. My poor choices enslaved me, and I freely lived under sin's bondage. Unfortunately, I chose to ignore the solution to all my problems by not knowing God's Word. It is my sincere prayer that God blesses you in all you say, think, and do. You should also deny yourself, take up your cross each day, and follow Jesus without ceasing.

Chapter 5

HUMILITY

First published in 1939, Alcoholics Anonymous "Big Book" was the work of one of the organization's founders. A man by the name of Bill Wilson was the one in question. Just before I went to prison for the first time in 2007. This was my first time attending an A. A. meeting at the North 40 Group in Fort Worth, Texas. The experience is as fresh in my memory as if it had happened yesterday. In Ft Worth, Texas, it was a hot day in August. At the meeting, most of the attendees were well dressed and friendly. There was something strange about it, because I felt as though I belonged. The people made me feel loved, needed, and wanted for the first time in my life. In order to please my second ex-wife, I attended the meeting on that day. At the ripe old age of twenty-nine, my life was at stake and in danger of being snuffed out.

In the end, I would succumb to the worst drug of all because of my addiction to alcohol. The drug in question was heroin. As I sat there with those alcoholics. It never occurred to me that I would become addicted to heroin one day! My knowledge of addiction was as limited as my knowledge of the Bible. It seemed to me that I had it all figured out. In addition to money, power, position, and prestige, I was gifted with a lot of talent that allowed me to earn a lot of money. While the recovering alcoholics provided each other with their experiences, strength, and hope, I listened intently. It's unfortunate that I didn't listen well enough and wasn't willing to change.

The people I met there were different from others I had encountered in my lifetime for some reason. The gleam in their eyes was indescribable. All of them laughed at themselves about the things they used to do in their past lives. A lot of Alcoholics Anonymous meetings conduct their meetings in a similar manner when there are newcomers present. They discussed Alcoholics Anonymous' first step. According to the first step, "We admit that we are powerless against alcohol and that life has become unmanageable for us."

RATIONALIZATION AND JUSTIFICATION

In one case, a man talked about waking up every morning and drinking six shots of Scotch before eating breakfast. Since he was shaking so badly from alcohol withdrawal, he spilled half of his first two shots before the alcohol took effect in his system, and then consumed the next four shots while getting dressed the next hour. After that, he could eat his breakfast. I remember sitting there and thinking to myself. The amount of alcohol I consume is not nearly as bad as these poor pitiful losers'. While I didn't drink every day like most people in the room, we still had a lot in common, even though I didn't drink every day. There was no difference between my life and that of the worst alcoholic in the room when it came to managing it. However, fate had other plans. In my mind, I rationalized and justified my drinking by saying I didn't drink every day.

It was impossible for me to quit drinking. However, something happened to me that day in that meeting. The fact that I didn't realize it at the time surprised me. The next time I went out, I started drinking. There was no way I could enjoy it anymore. There was never a time when I enjoyed drinking again. In a way, it was almost as if I knew I had a drinking problem but refused to admit it. My drinking problem was too serious to lie to myself any longer. Nevertheless, I believe I knew I was beat deep down. In retrospect, I wish I could talk to that extremely deceived young man who became the epitome of selfishness and self-centeredness, whose life was driven by fear, self-pity, self-deception, self-righteousness, and pride. My wish is to be able to share this with him. There was something beyond this world that he was looking for. He should also know that all the women, power, position, and prestige in this world will never fill that God-shaped void in his heart that he was trying to fill with the gods of this world. It would be my main message to myself that I was looking for God's love in Christ Jesus, not man's love.

I would also tell him that God is real and people matter in life. It would be nice if I could tell him that he should seek wisdom, knowledge, power, and understanding from God's word. The Creator of the universe is the only one who has all power, and I wish I could tell him that despite being powerless over his sin problem, there is someone who has all power and that person is Almighty God, the Creator of the universe. My heart longs to beg him to accept Jesus Christ as his Savior. It would be nice if I could tell him to repent, because the kingdom of Heaven is near. As a final wish, I would like to tell him that he should love God, his wife, and children with all his heart, until the day of his death. Ideally, I would give him the honesty, open-mindedness, and willingness to do everything that I have just described. Unfortunately, if I knew myself, I probably would not have listened.

I was the only guy on the planet that knew everything. But I knew absolutely nothing about life that mattered. I have to admit, as I got in my truck and drove off that day, the meeting did get me thinking. I thought about step one, of the twelve steps of Alcoholics Anonymous and what it meant for me to admit I was powerless. I didn't realize it at the time, but the good Lord was working behind the scenes to intervene and save my life. The good Lord definitely had his angels working overtime to protect me. I was slipping away into total darkness - a darkness that a lot of people don't come back from. That not even you in all your wildest dreams could ever imagine.

THE ROOT OF TROUBLE

The Bible talks about being unselfish like Christ in Philippians 2:5-8. According to the Bible, "In your lives you must think and act like

Christ Jesus" (Philippians 2:5, NIV, 2010). The Alcoholics Anonymous "Big Book" says, "Selfishness and self-centeredness are at the root of all our troubles" (World Services, 1939). There is no doubt in my mind that this is right. You already know how selfish and self-centered I was in my former life. I knew, however, that Jesus Christ was selfless. As a forty-one-year-old, my selfishness and self-centeredness led me down a path of self-destruction, straight to a self-induced tortures hell. As a result of my alcohol and drug use, all of this happened.

My selfishness and self-centeredness prevented me from seeing any of this. One day, a friend and mentor of mine was talking to me. I am referring to Dan Munger. This happened shortly after I made a commitment to Christ in 2018. Dan and I were talking about my life story. In response to my words, Dan looked at me straight in the eye and stopped for a brief moment. There was no doubt in my mind that Brother Dan was thinking. He chose his words very carefully, and I know it. As far as I know Dan, he strives to keep his conversation seasoned with grace. Dan knew at that moment that I had reached the depths of the grave and came back from it, as a result of my previous life. This is a consequence of not having Jesus check our sin problem. It is my belief that Dan knew I had spent so many years fighting everything in my life. He knew that it took me twenty-nine years of my life to learn how to admit I had been powerless over alcohol.

In truth, Dan also knew that my problem with alcohol was just a symptom of a deeper problem. I was addicted to sin because of my lack of faith! The Bible says, "We have all sinned and fallen short of the glory of God" (Romans 3:23, NIV, 2010). In my view, I was a sinner. Nevertheless, I didn't believe that God was entitled to run my life. As a result, I became the god of my own life, seated on the throne of selfishness and self-centeredness. Moreover, it made me very proud! The Bible says, "Pride goes before destruction, a haughty spirit before a fall" (Proverbs 16:18, NIV, 2010). The problem I had was sin, and if I didn't accept Jesus Christ as my savior, it would be worse. The consequences of my sin problem would cause me to die prematurely. A Bible verse states, "The wage of sin is death, but the gift of God is eternal life through Christ Jesus our Lord" (Romans 6:23, NIV, 2010). After hearing all the sermons, I had heard that Jesus loves me and has a plan for my life a million times. This had no effect on my life. I was the master of my life, the master of my world, and a fool as well.

It's also my belief that Dan knew that even though I was down, I wasn't out. It was obvious to Brother Dan at that moment that I only had one hope. In God's son Jesus Christ and the living God and Creator of all things. In his words, "The only way to overcome my self-centeredness and selfishness is to live a self-giving life." It had been my habit of living by self-propulsion for my whole former life, which had left me short of the life I was searching for, one full of meaning, one crowned with a sense of fulfillment, significance, and purpose.

My goal was to achieve a meaningful life and a true sense of happiness. Though I wasn't aware of it, I wanted and needed to be loved. Like Augustine, I also desired to have the God-shaped vacuum in my heart filled with God's love in Christ Jesus, or to put it another way, the void in my heart filled with God's love. My only desire, my only need was that. It is when we find God that we find a life full of meaning and purpose. There was a great deal of pain in my heart. My life was as empty as a beer bottle at three in the morning after a two-day binge.

THE RIGHT DECISION

In contrast to my former life, Dan's message of self-giving was exactly what I needed. A perfect moment in my life had arisen to say that. It wasn't apparent to me at the time. However, those words Dan spoke to me were from Almighty God himself, the Creator and Sustainer of life. I felt as though God himself had seared those words into my heart and mind with a branding iron at that moment. I made the conscious decision there and then to finally, after twenty-nine years, acknowledge that I was powerless over my addictions and compulsions, but what was most important, I realized I had a spiritual problem.

It was clear to me in the beginning that I was powerless over my sin problem and I was ready to do whatever it took to conquer it. After a lifetime of bad decisions and endless servitude, I finally bowed my head and followed Christ. It was only fitting that I do the next right thing in God's eyes, because the glory, honor, and praise that God deserves in my life and in all of creation are due to him. In addition, I decided to always do the right thing no matter how difficult the situation may be. It was time for me to put an end to doing the wrong thing in my life. In prayer before the Lord, I asked that he accept me as his servant.

This is impossible to believe! My father revealed to me that I was his son a few days later. My identity as a child of God was clear to me. It is written in the Bible, "The true children of God are those who let the Spirit lead them" (Romans 8:14, NIV, 2010). I began to follow what the Bible commands: "Anyone who wishes to follow me must deny himself, take up his cross, and follow me daily" (Luke 9:23, NIV, 2010). The Bible says, "In your lives you must act and think like Christ Jesus." After realizing I had no control over my sin problem, I then learned how not to even recognize my own existence. (6) Christ himself was like God in everything. But he did not think that being equal with God was something to be used for his own benefit. (7) But he gave up his place with God and made himself nothing. He was born to be a man and became like a servant. (8) And when he was living as a man, he humbled himself and was fully obedient to God, even when that caused his death-death on a cross" (Philippians 2:5-8, NIV, 2010). As a child of God, I realized I must deny myself and be humble in order to conform to Christ's measure and stature.

My former life was the epitome of selfishness and self-centeredness. It was right there in that moment, I made the decision that in my new life, I would be unselfish like Christ. I also ask God to allow me to be obedient to him, to the death like Christ was. It was from that moment forward that I had chosen to be faithful to the Lord. Obviously, I would do what God tells me to do since He is the God of my life as well as the commanding officer of my life, Jesus Christ. I made the decision to unconditionally trust in the Lord with all my heart.

I knew that the Bible said,"Love the Lord your God with all your heart, body, mind, soul, and strength. Furthermore it says,"Love patiently accepts all things. It always trusts, always hopes, and always remains strong" (1 Corinthians 13:4-5, NIV, 2010). So if I didn't trust God, I didn't love God, because love always trusts. In that moment I took my rightful place in creation for the first time in my life. I made it to my heavenly home, and my name was finally written in the lamb's book of life. A second realization occurred to me: love is an action. God gave something, and it was Jesus Christ. Ultimately, I concluded that I would give my life as a living sacrifice to God every day for all eternity.

I was studying the Bible intently and it became my way of staying close to the Lord. The Bible says, "Now the Lord is the Spirit, and where the Spirit of the Lord is, there is freedom" (2 Corinthians 3:17, NIV, 2010). In a matter of seconds, I come to this startling conclusion. The moment I confessed with my mouth that Jesus Christ is Lord, and believed in my heart that God raised him from the dead (Romans 10:9, Niv, 2010). In this moment, I recognized that I was blessed, saved, sanctified, redeemed, justified, and delivered by God. It is all by God's grace, which abounds to me, through Jesus Christ.

A SPIRITUAL MALADY

Looking back, I realized that I was powerless over my sin problem for the first time when I confessed this to God, myself, and another human being. I'm thankful that I realized that I was powerless over my addictions to drugs, alcohol, money, power, position, prestige, and anger. These are simply the facts! There was a deeper issue, which Dr. William Silkworth termed a spiritual malady. It was he who pioneered addiction science when little addiction science existed. At the beginning of the 1900s, he practiced medicine. He was speaking about a sin problem when he said "Spiritual Malady." At that moment I knew I had two choices: either treat the symptoms of my real problem and live a life of mediocrity, or treat my sin problem and live a life of excellence. The result would be an amazing life for me. My life would be full of happiness, joy, and eternal life. My realization of this liberated me from my sin problem and gave me a new life I almost died searching for. A life filled with significance, meaning, and purpose.

The Bible says, "So if I do things I do not want to do, then I am not the one doing them. It is sin living in me that does those things." (21) So, I have learned this rule: When I want to do good, evil is there with me. (22) In my mind, I am happy with God's law. (23) But I see another law working in my body, which makes war against the law my mind accepts. That other law working in my body is the law of sin, and it makes me its prisoner. So, in my mind I am a slave to God's law, but in my sinful self I am a slave to the law of sin" (Romans 7:20-23, NIV, 2010). In the end, I realized that after I had subscribed to a lifetime of self-destructive behavior. I needed to learn how to clothe myself in humility if I was going to have any quality of life. You need to understand something, humility doesn't mean you think less of yourself , it means you think of yourself less. That was my greatest problem in my former life, everything was about me.

One of the main reasons I was the King of Pride was the way I was raised. In addition to drinking heavily, my earthly father continually cursed at my mother, as well as fighting with her constantly. He was unable to show me or anybody else that he loved them. The way my father told me about my mistakes was by cursing and screaming. Most of the time, he was drunk when this happened. There was no positive reinforcement, not one good job, not one well done kid. As a result of that, I believed I wasn't good enough to be loved by my earthly father. This is a tragedy of the highest order!

It was a result of my ignorance of God's word, I couldn't resolve this love problem. It was my firm belief that God felt the same way toward me as well. My whole life felt like I was trying to prove that

I was worthy of love. Sadly, I did not receive the validation of being loved from my earthly father. As a result, I had no idea how to give or receive love. When someone truly loved me, based on what I now understand about love from God. That is, unconditionally. Unfortunately, I wasn't able to accept it. It was impossible for me to accept anything, even the simplest thing, such as a hug. The reason for this was because I have felt unloved, unneeded, and unwanted my entire life. There was nothing I could do to accept someone's love for me, no matter what they did for me.

DESPERATE FOR APPROVAL

It was imperative that I had the approval of my father in order to succeed. I was devastated when I didn't get his approval and love. As a result, I became obsessed with the things of this world and the love of money. This thought process nearly ended my life. I realized in the end that success doesn't depend on your bank account balance. It's all about how many quality relationships you have. It was crucial for me to hear my father telling me he loved me and approves of me. A lack of love and approval from my father would have made me feel like I was the poorest person on Earth, no matter how rich I was. There is nothing worse than for a child to experience this. There was no difference between my father putting a gun to my head and pulling the trigger! Ultimately, this was the factor that sent me spiraling out of control. The saddest part of all of this is? My father used to tell me stories about his father treating him the same way. In the same way he made me feel, my father felt the same way. It was his father who made him feel that way as well.

The true transformation came after surrendering my life to the Lord, renewing my mind through the word of God, and having the mind of Christ. My search for love, peace, and joy lasted many years. My understanding of God's love was finally clarified when I learned that it can be received through Jesus Christ's sacrifice. My humility would actually enable me to say, "Lord, let your kingdom come, and your will be done in my life as it is in heaven." It took me a lifetime of heartache and pain to realize what the Bible was talking about when it says, "But God commendeth his love toward us, in that, while we were yet sinners, Christ died for us." (Romans 5:8, NIV, 2010). That is, Christ died for us despite the fact that we lived against God and deserved to be punished in some way. My message to you is that Christ died for us, at the time we weren't good enough, at the time we were dead in our sins. As humanity had fallen into brokenness, God poured out his love, grace, and mercy upon us through his son Jesus. Those words in Romans 5:8 were the catalyst that changed my life. As I surrendered and renewed my mind through the word of God, I realized I was complete only after being filled with God's love through Christ Jesus.

My pride, anger, hatred, bitterness, and unforgiveness still plagued me, even after I admitted that I could not control my sin problem. You heard me say that I was the proudest man on Earth, and I believed that God had forgiven me for all the sins I had committed against him. Sadly, as a result of my ignorance of the Bible and foolish pride. This prevented me from fully receiving God's forgiveness. The things I did to people and the person I had become were just too much for me to forgive. I say this with all due respect for my father, I promised myself that I would never be like him.

My father was a better man than I ever imagined he would be, and he did the best he could with the life skills he had. It is not my intention to give you the wrong impression of my father. Despite his shortcomings, he wasn't a bad person. As I was in my former life, he had trouble giving or receiving love. My point in all of this is that when I was a child, I swore I would never be like him. The verdict is in, and I was right. I abandoned my wife and children twenty-four times, I was worse than my father on his worst day.

FORGIVE YOURSELF

In total, nearly seventeen years of prison time was required for three out of twenty-four arrests. In the end, I had a very negative self-image. My decision to leave my wife and children for prison caused me to view myself as a deserter of the worst kind. This way of thinking leads you to fall into the oldest trick in the book by the enemy, which is refusing to accept God's forgiveness completely. As a result of this line of thinking, we judge ourselves and play the role of god. Moreover, I am not just living in sin. Additionally, I am constantly subjected to guilt, shame, and condemnation. The consequence of my judgment of myself instead of receiving God's grace is this. It is essentially saying, "I thank God for forgiving me for all of my sins, but I cannot forgive myself." Then I'm telling God, "I won't accept your forgiveness, let alone submit to your will. I'm the god of my life." It is kind of like this. Your child asks you for twenty dollars to go to the movies. You hand your child a twenty-dollar bill, and tell him, "Have a great time." Then he looks at you and says, "I cannot take that, I didn't work for it." Would you not be confused? There's no doubt in my mind that you would! We do exactly that when we deny God's forgiveness in any area of our lives. There is a key point here: it is you who is confused about the process of forgiveness, but God is not.

Therefore, we need to be clothed in humility to accept that we are not worthy, but God is a worthy recipient of praise, glory, and honor. In order for God to take his rightful position in your life, you must clothe yourself in humility like Christ did. The blood of Jesus purchased God's forgiveness for us so that we may be blessed with unconditional love, grace, and mercy. As a condition of receiving God's forgiveness, I must also forgive myself. If I do not forgive myself, then God's grace has been received in vain. I never imagined it would be as easy as receiving God's grace through Christ alone. Honestly, I believed that I had to atone for the atrocities I committed against people in the past before I could be saved by God's amazing grace. A definition of grace is an unmerited favor. It is unearned and I know that now. It is also my understanding that we can receive his grace at any time, and if we are waiting for our works to get to Heaven, we will never reach it. The Bible says, "For it is by grace you have been saved, through faith—and this is not from yourselves, it is the gift of God—not by works, so that no one can boast" (Ephesians 2:8-9, NIV, 2010).

In truth, when I rebelled against God, I had no idea how my sin would affect me spiritually. Although I knew right from wrong, until I gave my life to the Lord in 2018, I could not see things clearly from a spiritual perspective. I also couldn't believe that I was worthy of God's grace because of my poor self-image and ignorance of the word of God. It took me a long time to realize that if I was waiting for a better resume to get into Heaven, I would never make it.

LIFE ON GOD'S TERMS

It is important to live life on God's terms, which God's Word taught me. As Jesus said long ago, "Deny yourself, take up your cross, and follow him every day" (Luke 9:23, NIV, 2010). My problem was that I considered my Heavenly Father to be the same way I perceived my earthly father. In my heart, I believed that I had to be good enough to be loved, needed, and wanted. I also believed that less sin was required of me. First, I needed to think differently. In order for God to accept me and offer me his grace, I had to do better. As I studied God's Word every day, I became more and more devoted to it. The more I read, I became deeply captivated by God's nature. The Bible says "Take hold of my words with all your heart; keep my commands, and you will live. Get wisdom, get understanding; do not forget my words or turn away from them" (Proverbs 4:5, NIV, 2010).

After reading the Bible for a while, I was stunned when it said "But the gift is not like the trespass. For if the many died by the trespass of the one man, how much more did God's grace and the gift that came by the grace of the one man, Jesus Christ, overflow to the many! (Romans 5:15, NIV, 2010). In the very same chapter it says, "Christ died for us while we were sinners" (Romans 5:6, NIV, 2010). At that moment, I realized that my pride was preventing me from receiving God's grace on a daily basis because of my ignorance of God's word. Once I received affirmation from God through his word, I never again had problems receiving his grace, or as I prefer to call it, his unmerited favor.

IDOL OF SELF

The great thing about knowing that is that I can clothe myself in humility every day. A humble heart is prepared to receive God's grace, to do his will, and to complete his work, all to God's glory. My life has been profoundly affected by the fact that this grace is a free gift from God and that it was bought and paid for with the blood of Jesus Christ. My attitude of gratitude, my freedom from self, and most importantly, the fact that it is free, it is unmerited, makes me fall in love with God deeper and deeper every time I think about it. As a result, I am kept off the throne and God is allowed to take his rightful place in my life every day. My biggest idol in my lifetime took me twenty-nine years and a lot of heartache and pain to remove from power. Idol number one was self. Every day, I pray that the Lord would have mercy on those who set themselves up as their own god. The worst idol of all is the idol of self.

The main motto of my former life was "me first." People throughout history have been referred to as the "me first" generation. A very important teaching of Jesus for living in his kingdom is based on this tendency. He will give the last place in his kingdom to those who give themselves first place in this life. Likewise, those who give themselves the lowest place by placing others first will be given first place (Matthew 23:11-12, NIV, 2010). A good friend and mentor of mine, Brother Dan Munger, listened to my testimony for the first time in 2019 and after I finished he looked straight at me and said, "You have to be of maximum service to God and others." That is what Jesus was saying in the Bible, in the book of Matthew 23:11-12. It was important for me to serve God and others with the right motive in my heart.

In all things, I must keep in mind that "God is worthy." There is a time for serving others, but it is not for their benefit, it is for the benefit of God's kingdom. This is the pure motive of our hearts that God wants from us. As I realized this, I came to this conclusion, and that is God deserves all the glory in my life. It is impossible to realize this without humility. Since I grasped the importance of this verse, I have lived a humble life day after day, having learned that the only way to gain God's grace is by living a life of humility. I believe that is the absolute truth. The only way to receive God's grace is through humility, which is the garment of Christ.

THE WAY OF HUMILITY

As I realized for the first time in my life, I could never be good enough to receive God's grace without accepting Jesus Christ as my personal savior. In my former life, I had lost everything that had made it worth living and the end result was that I had lost everything I was proud of. In addition to my mother's death, my father became crippled and I was unable to help him even when he needed it most, my aunt, the only person who was connected to my mother, died one month after my mother, and my eldest brother is still addicted to heroin to this day and dying from liver cancer. After my mother died in 2020, my younger brother became addicted to methamphetamine. Lastly, the courts would terminate my parental rights to my youngest daughter, who is my heart and soul. It wasn't even possible for me to say goodbye to her. The last, but certainly not the least. As of today, I am still wanted in three counties in Texas. The more I realize how powerless I am in every arena of my life today, the more I am humbled. Nevertheless, it is my Lord and my God who has all the power, and he calls me back to him day after day through humility. As we go through each day, I believe that's God's way of keeping us dependent on him.

It is my goal and my dream that when God gets me out of this mess I have created through my own selfishness and self-centeredness, that I will preach the gospel to people from all over the world and on every continent. In a situation like this, I don't know how God is going to get me out of it. Nevertheless, I am certain that I will fulfill my destiny by God's grace. There is no doubt that God will make that happen. The man I am today is a different one from the one I was yesterday. Through Jesus Christ and God's word, the Bible, we are a new creation. My life has changed for the better because I realize there is no barrier to a person coming to Christ, no matter what their background or where they come from. The reason God loves us is because he created us. There is never a moment when I don't thank God for my relationship with him, and my fellow man. God kept his word, so here I am, just as I am. The truth is, I am a faithful slave of Christ, and I thank God for that. Also, I am grateful that I have reached my Heavenly home.

Chapter 6

GOD, SELF, OR SATAN

It was a typical day in the Hancock County Jail. I had just completed a sixteen-hour workday. I fought all day to get to the classes I taught on time. There were ten students waiting for me in the back classroom of the jail ready to go to Chainbreakers. Chainbreakers is an in-house drug and alcohol rehabilitation program that meets for three hours a day, for thirty days straight. In 2019, Dan and Joan Munger started the program at the Hancock County Jail under Sheriff Ricky Adam's leadership.

The new class had just started. I was teaching Chainbreaker's rehab class for the third time. When I finished my introduction, I pointed at the dry erase board and said, "The disease of addiction is treated on three fronts. The first is the evidentiary side, which takes into account the biology of addiction. In addition to Cognitive Behavioral Therapy, the spiritual side is also important, since addiction is a spiritual illness. Cognitive Behavioral Therapy teaches us that our thoughts determine our emotions, attitudes, and actions." I then paused and pointed to it again. I said, "It must have been repeated to me a million times in my former life that, if I wanted to change my actions, I had to change my thinking. It is indeed true, but it is much more difficult than you would expect." My former way of life, I didn't realize one factor, that when you don't know the truth, you choose to live a lie. This is true because for twenty-nine years I chose to ignore the Word of God and live a lie instead. It all boils down to the fact that the Word of God is the absolute truth about everything in creation and you can't change your behavior without changing your thinking.

The Word of God contains the truth and the answer to all of humanity's problems; if you choose to ignore the truth, that is no excuse in the eyes of God for living a lie. When you default and live a lie, the father of your lies is Satan, because Satan is the father of pride and lies. There is one thing for certain in this life: you will either serve Almighty God or Satan. In this case, there are no gray areas. The results of serving God through Jesus Christ are: love, joy, peace, patience, kindness, generosity, faithfulness, gentleness, self-control and righteousness. It is only by knowing the Word of God that you will be able to stand for the truth. It allows you to live a life filled with meaning, purpose, and significance. Your choice to serve Satan will lead you to live a lie, stay unrighteous, live-in darkness, sin, sickness, and death. Today, humanity is manifesting two things: God or Satan, and if you don't deny yourself, Satan is your father. There is no doubt in my mind that this is the truth. In this case, it is a matter of life and death, light and darkness, lies and the truth, faith and fear. Who will you serve, God or self and Satan?

It was ignorance of the Word of God, stubbornness, and blatant outright rebellion against God that motivated me in my former life to serve Satan's purposes faithfully to the point of almost literally dying for their sake. I want you to understand this fundamental Bible truth in layman's terms: "You will deny yourself/die to self or die in your sins," according to the Bible. You have the choice between life and death, so follow Christ and choose life. I received the general outline of this book's content from God in three minutes before I wrote it. At this point, you're probably wondering, what in the world does that have to do with anything? The point is, in order to listen to God, you have to know his voice. You can only know God's voice through understanding His nature, which comes from knowing the Bible. As a result, this contributes to the shaping of your identity in Christ, as well as bringing you to the measure and stature of Christ. It is through the way of humility, you can deny yourself, and keep your life dedicated to God. I figured out what I'm telling you after years of serving Satan's purposes and living a lie. This is something you need to get down in your soul. Your thoughts, which direct your emotions and attitudes, and produce your actions, always come from three sources. They can come from God, yourself, or Satan. Your duty is to control them based on the truths of the Bible.

HOLD EVERY THOUGHT CAPTIVE

As Christians, we are told throughout the Bible how to conduct ourselves, think, and behave. One verse in the New Testament says, "We demolish arguments and every pretension that sets itself up against the knowledge of God, and we take captive every thought to make it obedient to Christ" (2 Corinthians 10:5, NIV, 2010). Essentially, God was telling us to think about what we are thinking and to disregard everything that does not align with the Word of God.

Usually, people are either ignorant of God's Word or choose to act on what the enemy tells them to think about or do. As a result, they live in a defeated mindset. It used to be that my mind was the scariest neighborhood I had ever been in, which was why I had so many problems in my former life. My ignorance of biblical truth prevented me from knowing truth from lies. Since I didn't know the truth, I made very poor choices and ended up living a lie ad infinitum. As a result, I was unable to make good decisions based on the truth, since I was ignorant of it. You cannot know what life is really about if you don't know the Bible's absolute truth. Our lack of knowledge about the truth also causes us a lot of unnecessary suffering.

I know and believe that people try their best with the mentality they have. The problem is when you don't know the Word of God, you are susceptible to falling for anything. The good news is that if you know the biblical truth about something, you still have the power to make the right decision for the situation at hand. It would then be icing on the cake if we act in faith, pleasing the Lord. As I see it, God has put us in an ideal win/win situation by giving us Bible truth, as well as the ability to apply it to our lives. The Bible does not lie, so we can never go wrong by knowing and applying it.

It is impossible to please the Lord if you don't know God's Word, because your faith will not be anchored in the right place. There should never be a point in which your faith should be in anyone or anything other than God. According to the Bible, "That faith is the substance of things hoped for and evidence of things not yet seen" (Hebrews 11:1, NIV, 2010). Furthermore, the Bible says, "And without faith it is impossible to please God, because anyone who comes to him must believe that he exists and that he rewards those who earnestly seek him" (Hebrews 11:6, NIV, 2010). It is now apparent to me that my cognitive behavior determines everything. As a Christian, it is vital that my mind and thought processes be renewed by God's Word. It's crucial that I learn about life and what comes after this one. It is also necessary for me to know the truth about God, myself, and Satan.

As I gained an accurate understanding of the Bible, I realized I could be freed from the shackles of sin, self, and Satan! We cannot accomplish this on our own, regardless of how hard we try. Our faith must be rooted in God through his son Jesus Christ and we must be willing to surrender our lives to him one moment at a time, one day at a time. The way this happens is by holding every thought captive and bringing it into the obedience of Christ. The Bible says, "For as he reckoneth/thinks within himself, so is he" (Proverbs 23:7, NIV, 2010). The Word of God not only transforms us when we renew our minds with it, but it also transforms our whole lives.

According to King David in the book of Psalms, "I have hidden your word in my heart that I might not sin against you" (Psalms 119:11, NIV, 2010). This is what happens when we renew our minds through God's Word. There is a whole new way of thinking about things. Our spiritual heart is affected by this thought process, which makes our motives towards God and others pure. Thus, we transform our ungodly emotions, attitudes, and actions into Godly ones. The next time you get distracted, remember what I said about Cognitive Behavior: the thoughts we think dictate the emotions we feel and the attitudes we have, in other words, our spiritual heart, which is what determines our actions. In the eyes of Almighty God, the motives of the heart are everything. The motives of our heart begin in our thinking, which should begin and end with God"s infallible Word.

I told you there are 850 references in the Bible to the heart. Furthermore, the Bible refers to the heart twice as the one that pumps blood out of 850 occurrences. The Bible refers to the core of one's being when it talks about the heart. My aim is to get you to see that you need to change your thinking, to change your actions. Furthermore, repentance and changing your thoughts, by applying the Word of God to your thinking, changes your path from the broad way that many are on, and leads to death. The Word of God keeps you on the narrow path that leads to life everlasting. It is important for you to understand this fundamental truth because "Those who do what the Father requires will go to Heaven" (Matthew 7:21, NIV, 2010).

SIGNS OF A FOLLOWER

It is written, "Not everyone who says to me, 'Lord, Lord,' will enter the kingdom of heaven, but only the one who does the will of my Father who is in heaven. Many will say to me on that day, 'Lord, Lord, did we not prophesy in your name and in your name drive out demons and in your name perform many miracles?' Then I will tell them plainly, 'I never knew you. Away from me, you evildoers' (Matthew 7:21-23, NIV, 2010). In order to be a hearer and doer of God's Word, you need to know the Word of God, or you will not be able to apply it to your life.

A person who does not obey God's word is not doing what the Father requires, and so he or she will not go to heaven. The Bible says, "Whoever says, "I know him," but does not do what he commands is a liar, and the truth is not in that person" (1 John 2:4, NIV, 2010). It is very important that you understand these two passages completely. It doesn't have to do with works either. What I'm referring to is the kind of repentance that keeps you coming back, repenting and believing every day. It's basically a measure of surrender where you give God the freedom and power to do his will through you on a daily basis. This is the godly sorrow that leads to a true repentance and salvation without regret, the Apostle Paul was talking about in (2 Corinthians 7:10, NIV, 2010).

In retrospect, I realize that for a new Christian who doesn't know a whole lot about the Bible. There is a lot of importance in this topic, and this goes for addicts, criminals, rich or poor people who have a defeated mentality, or some would say, a carnal mind, and don't know what they are lacking in life. It's important that you never forget what I'm going to tell you. It doesn't matter who you are, or where you're from. Every person needs Jesus, whether they are in prison, in a penthouse on Park Avenue, or a homeless addict sleeping on a park bench. The Lord Jesus Christ is the answer! It is in Jesus that we find victory!

It is clear in (Romans 12:1) that God's Word must be imparted to the mind if we want to experience true transformation. There is one thing I will always remember about my former life, which is this one fact, that for twenty-nine years, I lived with an oh poor pitiful me mentality. It was not until the day I almost lost life itself that I realized what a precious gift life truly is! My world was as big as the gifts I gave to God's creation. In the end, there was nothing to be found, because I gave nothing. This was something I realized only after I began renewing my mind with God's infallible Word and living a self-giving life.

My ignorance of God's Word caused me to become the most selfish, self-centered, and proud human being on earth. My freedom and victory today are purely a result of knowing God's Word. The living Word, Jesus, the Bible, and the power of the Holy Spirit made all of this possible. As a result of my accurate knowledge of these three things, I am free today. If you believe something, even if it's a lie, it's your truth. The way I thought in my former life always led me down the path of self-destruction. I knew nothing else. It is only by God's grace and a renewed mind that we can be true followers of Christ.

THE ONLY SOLUTION

The sad truth about my former life was that my value was derived from people, places, and things. It would be highly recommended that you avoid playing such a game. In the long run, it will leave you feeling constantly devalued and lead to frustration and disappointment. I suffered from all kinds of problems because I did not know the truths of the Bible. After six shots of heroin a day, I quickly realized this startling fact. If you don't have a clear understanding of the Bible and you continue to live a lie, you will die in your sin.

There is one solution to all of humanity's problems in all of creation: the living Word, which is Jesus, and the inerrant Word, which is the Bible. The amazing thing about this line of thinking is that true believers in Christ and humanity itself confirm it. Likewise, my past and present experiences confirm this. My former thoughts were similar to this. As I constantly degraded myself, I would say, "You are a deserter, you abandoned your kids and wife to go party with strippers." There was also another line that stuck in my mind: "I can't do that because I'm a felon, I'm too good to serve other people, people should serve me." These lines played constantly in my head. It would have been better if I had done this, if only I had done that, if only she would have acted differently. The world would be a better place if my parents had more money and were different.

My current perspective on that mentality makes me laugh. The reason for this is because I no longer have a victim's mentality. My mind has been renewed with God's Word, so I have a victor's mentality. It is a victor's mentality that tells me over and over again that I am needed, loved, and wanted by the Most High God. There is no one else like me on Earth, that I am unique and special, and that no one can replace me. My existence is the result of the Creator of the universe breathing life into me. I am God's workmanship, created in Christ Jesus to do good works which he prepared for me before I was born. As long as Christ strengthens me, I will be able to accomplish all things. I have the capacity, the equipment, and the strength to accomplish what God has assigned to me. When God is on my side, who can stand against me? Today, I constantly remember that greater is He who is in me than he who is in the world. Currently, a new recording is playing in my mind that says, "I am more than a conqueror in Christ Jesus." There is a transformation of the human mind that occurs when it is renewed by the Word of Almighty God. You can change your heart and life by surrendering your life to the Lord, coming to a true repentance, and renewing your mind with the word of God.

Do you have any idea how I felt when I lived with a defeated mentality? As a result of a negative thought process. The way I talked to myself for years was downright condescending. My faith was in the lies that Satan himself told me, the "Great Deceiver." My belief was based on the lies that others told me and that Satan himself told them. Through Satan's influence, I spoke lies over other people's lives. After a long journey, I finally realized that Satan, the oldest slickster in this game called life, had greatly deceived me. I was Satan's whore, being used to project evil against my fellow man, myself, and all that I did was designed to destroy me and others.

BELIEVING ISN'T ENOUGH

The worst part of it was I knew that Jesus was the answer the whole time. Throughout my life, I have believed in God, Jesus, and the cross. However, simply believing won't suffice. The Bible says "You believe there is one God. Good! But the demons believe, and they tremble with fear" (James 2:19, NIV, 2010). As I have mentioned before, I have believed in God since I was 5 years old, even going so far as to say the sinner's prayer of repentance. In other words, if believing is enough, what was I doing wrong? Why did I almost die? What was I thinking when I created so much trouble for myself? Essentially, I had not reached a godly sorrow that leads to true repentance and salvation without regret.

Generally speaking, the sinner's prayer was sincere on my part. As I confessed with my mouth that Jesus is Lord, I also believed in my heart that He had been raised from the dead by God. Through faith, I knew and believed I was saved by God's amazing saving grace. There is only one channel, and that is faith, and not by works. As a result of the spiritual malady/sin problem, I accepted the treatment. There was one important detail I forgot to include. It is a two fold process when you repent. When we become a Christian, you repent from your heart and mind. In my heart, I repented, however, I had not renewed my carnal mind through God's word. It is for this reason that there was no external transformation. Consequently, I still lived defeated, as I remained ignorant of God's Word. I therefore lived in bondage by the choices I made because I was ignorant of Bible truth, which meant I had no choice but to live a lie. Our faith will motivate our actions to serve God, when we believe God's Word.

MAKING TIME FOR GOD

My greatest amazement is that the average person is awake for 16 hours a day. Sadly, they cannot find an hour to spend with the Lord studying his Word. There is something deeply troubling about that. I'm certain that our Heavenly Father must also be feeling the same way, as we were all made for a relationship with him through his son Jesus Christ, and to glorify him through relationships with others. God's Word is the absolute truth; it gives us another choice, one that frees us from the bonds of self by not living a lie. God's words will not return to him void.

Previously, I lived life the way Jesus talked about leading to death, when I thought the way I used to. As is common among most people today, I made every excuse for not reading the Bible. There was always something else I needed to do. I realize now that all that I wanted was for my earthly father to spend time with me, just as our Heavenly Father wants us to spend time with him studying his Word, doing his will, and completing his work, by humbly offering our bodies as a living sacrifice to him.

Interestingly, the transformation that comes by the renewing of the mind would have changed my life and saved me, my wife, children, and family a lot of heartache and pain. The truth is that I lied to myself and said I did not have time to read the Bible. However, I made time to inject heroin six times a day, I got drunk, I went to strip clubs, I went to professional baseball games, I went to at least six concerts a year. The problem was that I hardly had any time for Jesus. My sole purpose in attending church was to feel better about myself. The reason I went to church and prayed is that I wanted something from Jesus. Since I was consumed by myself in my former life, I would never have attended church for the right reasons. The reason why is because I didn't know God or his Word. I regret to say that's the cold hard truth.

I am alive today because of God's amazing grace. The first thing I do each morning is ask God to give me knowledge of his will and the power to carry it out. My morning starts with saying what the Apostle Paul said, "In view of God's mercy, I offer my body as a living sacrifice. For this is my spiritual act of worship" (Romans 12:1, NIV, 2010). A Christian's life is such a blessing because they are able to have their minds renewed by the Word of God and see God working in their lives, as well as those around them. It is a blessing to me that I can glorify God with my life in this way on a daily basis. I believe God is worthy of my worship, so this is important to me.

In truth, Jesus never meant to sell tickets on the guilt trip. You must understand that salvation is a supernatural act. The process is preceded and followed by repentance. As a matter of fact, the gospels were written in Greek and the word "repent" was recorded as "metanoia." The word "Meta" means "after" and it bears the concept of "shift" or "change" (as in the word metamorphosis). The word "Noia" translates to "mind." Moreover, repentance in (Hebrew: תשובה, literally, "return", pronounced tshuva or teshuva) is one element of atoning for sin in Judaism. This is something you should never forget! It is impossible to live a life of victory and repent if your thoughts are not changed by God's Word. The act of repentance includes this. You must never forget that even if you repent from the depths of your heart, if you don't renew your mind with the Word of God, you won't see any change in your life, because your mind hasn't changed. This is so crucial for you to understand because repentance is two fold. We must repent from our hearts and minds. It is when we do this that God takes his rightful place in our lives. We can't truly repent without having our minds renewed with God's word. It is imperative that we turn our ungodly thoughts into Godly thoughts, which, in turn, dictate Godly emotions/attitudes that lead to Godly actions. A relationship with God cannot be established through Jesus Christ if you do not know the nature of God because you have not spent the time to study the Bible carefully.

The situation reminds me of when I pursued a relationship with my first wife. She and I talked twice a day and I found out what she liked and disliked. As she spoke, I listened intently. It is safe to say that I studied every move she made. I took my time and did this in order to make sure I wanted to be in a relationship with her, because if I'm going to marry her, I'll need to know what she expects from me. In the same way, our relationship with God through Jesus Christ is similar. My relationship with God must be based on a knowledge of who He is and what He requires of me. "Those who do what the Father requires go to Heaven" (Matthew 7:21-23, NIV, 2010).

My former life was characterized by believing in God, but that's not enough. The book of James clearly says, "You believe that there is one God. Good! Even the demons believe that—and shudder. You foolish person, do you want evidence that faith without deeds is useless? Was not our father Abraham considered righteous for what he did when he offered his son Isaac on the altar? You see that his faith and his actions were working together, and his faith was made complete by what he did" (James 2:19-22, NIV, 2010).

It's easy to understand this verse if I break it down for you. Our faith grows as we study God's Word, so that we can do what is pleasing in God's sight. We achieve this through our measure of surrender and the work of the Holy Spirit. Our actions need to be changed in order to achieve this. There is a need for me to change my Cognitive Behavior. Therefore, I need to change the way I think by studying the Bible.

As a result, not only do I renew/change my mind, but I get transformed as well. In addition to gaining more faith, I'm acting based on faith, which pleases God. The Bible says, "Faith comes by hearing and hearing the word of Christ" (Romans 10:17, NIV, 2010). Remember that the Bible says, "And without faith it is impossible to please God, because anyone who comes to him must believe that he exists and that he rewards those who earnestly seek him." The Bible teaches us that in order to grow in faith, to please God, we must study the Bible and renew our minds. Our hearts and lives must be transformed through God's Word. It is impossible to achieve transformation unless we change our cognitive behavior. Everyone who claims to be a Christian must renew his or her mind. It's the most important component for a true follower of Christ.

In reality, without changing your thinking, without changing your perception from a biblical perspective, you forever default to living a lie. The reason for this is because you don't know the absolute truth about life and cannot take your rightful place in God's creation. Furthermore, you cannot enter God's kingdom. As the Bible states, "When we come to Christ and are transferred from the kingdom of darkness to the kingdom of light by way of Jesus Christ, then we become ambassadors of Christ, pilgrims, sojourners." Ambassadors are people who live and represent other nations in foreign countries. The purpose of our existence on earth is to glorify our Heavenly Father, our home is Heaven. An ambassador for God cannot exist without understanding God's nature through the living Word of God, Jesus, the Bible, and the Holy Spirit of Truth. In order to represent God, I must renew my mind through the Word of God. This is the only way to achieve it.

In all you acquire, you should gain wisdom, knowledge, and understanding of God's Word. It is also important to get in agreement with God's Word, regardless of how good or how bad your life has turned out. Then, when you are converted to Christ, you need to renew your mind with God's Word and come to a full repentance. God can then be exalted in and through you by the power of his Holy Spirit, which is determined by the measure of surrender you demonstrate. Whenever you surrender, God's power flows to and through you to glorify him, and then God is able to do for you what you are unable to do for yourself. You are the most important thing He can use to help others.

SPIRIT-POWERED

Consequently, the Word of the Lord says, "'Not by might nor by power, but by my Spirit,' says the LORD Almighty." (Zechariah 4:6, NIV, 2010). You can achieve anything when you have God in you, working according to his will and good pleasure. A true child of God who walks not after the flesh, but after the Spirit, will overcome anything and everything in Heaven, on Earth, under the Earth, and even all the forces of Hell can't stop them! The Apostle Paul said, "It is not I who lives, but Christ who lives in me, and the life I live, I live by faith in the son of God because he loved and gave himself for me" (Galatians 2:20, NIV, 2010). The concept of true repentance was taught to me in this way. According to my understanding, Paul's letter to the Galatians was written to defend the Gospel of grace and justification by faith. As Paul wrote Galatians, he aimed to combat legalistic corrupters of the simple Good News of salvation by grace through faith.

When I first accepted Christ as my Savior at the age of twelve, I was sincere. In humility, I confessed with my mouth that Jesus Christ is Lord and believed in my heart that God raised Him from the dead. My heart was open to receiving Jesus. However, I was not regenerated by God's Word and the power of the Holy Spirit. In my ignorance of God's Word, I perpetually lived a lie, serving Satan's purposes, and caused a lot of problems in my life. Based on the Bible, I did not change my perception. My main problem was that I did not know the truth, so I fell for any purpose Satan presented.

It was my defeated mentality and my carnal mind that caused me to love the world. In the Bible it says, "So, you are not loyal to

God! You should know that loving the world is the same as hating God. Anyone who wants to be a friend of the world becomes God's enemy." (5) God opposes the proud, but he gives his grace to the humble" (James 4:4-5, NIV, 2010). I can attest to these two verses for 41 years in my former life. My former life was filled with worldliness, and I would say "I love God with my lips, but deny him with my actions." This was just like what Adam and Eve did in the Garden of Eden. This mentality made me become the proudest man on the planet because I said, "I believe in you God, but you don't have the right to run my life." That set me up as the god of my life. These actions led me into the depths of darkness from which most people never recover. I was opposed by God when I became proud. My good fortune was that God was merciful to me and kept calling me back through humility.

SELF-INDUCED TORTURES HELL

I am so grateful and thankful that God spared my life, which belonged to him anyways long before I became its manager or steward. My love for Jesus led me to obey his commandments after I converted to Christianity. Sadly, I loved the idea of him in my former life. As a result of my ignorance of God's Word, I failed to demonstrate my love for him through my actions. My ignorance of God's Word led me to believe lies and serve Satan's purposes faithfully for twenty-nine years. I kept living in bondage as a result of that, which reduced my life to a meager existence. A self-imposed prison then formed around me, and I experienced tortures like you could never imagine.

The end result was that I ended up with $1,380.00 in cash and a whole lot of wasted talent. There are a lot of Christians that fail to recognize their identity in Christ when they have not repented from their heart and from their mind. The key to transformation is to change your perception from a biblical perspective. The key to changing your actions is to change your thinking. Regardless of whether you live in the light or the darkness, in bondage or in freedom, you will either be a slave to righteousness, or to sin. The choice is ours as Christians, to learn the truth of the Bible and walk in victory. There are a lot of Christians today living in defeat. We are transformed from the inside out when we choose to follow Jesus and renew our minds with God's Word. We transform as new creatures through our thoughts, emotions, attitudes, and actions. If you want to achieve this, you will need to surrender your life to Christ one day at a time and do it through Jesus Christ and God's Word.

VICTOR'S MENTALITY ABOUT SCARS

All I could think about were my scars, my past, and how much I regret everything that had happened. Similarly, I kept living in a defeatist mentality because I refused to listen to the Word of the Most High God. The will of God was not something I would submit to. I knew life was tough, and we couldn't live too long without getting injured or experiencing some kind of pain or suffering. A wound can sometimes heal up and leave no trace of its existence. When wounds are so severe, because they're so deep, they heal but leave scars on the body. People I knew, including myself, had scars from falling off a bike as a child, from surgeries to remove illnesses, and from accidents. As well as physical scars, there are also invisible scars. These scars are the result of inner wounds, from divorce, from what somebody said, or from mistakes we have made. It is so common for us to hide our scars that we don't see anything positive about them. As we look at these scars, we remember the pain, the tragedy, and the betrayal that we have undergone. Our wish is for them to disappear.

In order to transform our thinking about scars, we need to see them in a new light. God did not allow scars to discourage us. We are reminded of what he has brought us through because of it. Basically, we received God's grace in order to get through it. It took me thirty-one years to be able to look at my scars and not see the pain. As a result, it is a way to reflect on the grace of God as you look at them. When you have a scar, it means that the wound has healed, it means that the pain has passed and you are on your way to recovery. The scar signifies that what kept you awake at night is behind you now. You don't need to become bitter and live a life of regret.

Your transformed way of thinking, as a result of God's Word, can change the way you view that scar. Another way of putting it is that your victor's mentality can change the way you look at the scar. Your scar is a testament to God's faithfulness, and without his mercy that mistake could have stopped your progress. That illness could have caused death if not for his healing. It's easy to get discouraged and believe an obstacle is insurmountable. When you see that scar, say to God, "You healed me back then, you restored my marriage, you helped me overcome the loss of my loved one." The experience wasn't easy, but this scar will serve as a reminder of your goodness to me. The same thing you did for me back then is what I know and believe you will do for me now. Through a biblical perspective, you can use your scars as fuel for your faith if you view them in the right way. As you see them, you will be reminded of God's love, grace, mercy, and goodness.

In the past few years, I have learned that it is not necessary to hide your scars. What you've been through doesn't have to embarrass you. When viewed in a Godly manner, your scars can be an asset rather than an obstacle. A fascinating aspect of the Bible is that no one in the scriptures accomplished their destiny without scars. Things happen in life that we didn't expect and we all get hurt. Our health is unexpectedly impacted by illness, a family member dies suddenly, we make mistakes, and people come against us. Furthermore, if you are going to fulfill your destiny. Don't be depressed over what you have been through. Don't wallow in self-pity because it wasn't fair. It is important that you choose a new perspective. In spite of the enemy's attempts to stop you, God healed you. What makes you so sure? There is a scar to prove it. There is no need to feel ashamed of your scars, nor are you depressed over them, because you are at peace with them. It was God's hand protecting you from the opposition. It is not your scars that remind you of the pain, it is the scars that remind you of the greatness of God.

Your enemy was unable to take you out, sure there is a scar, and sure it hurt. It is wonderful that you have survived and come out of it healed, restored, vindicated, blessed, and fulfilling your purpose. It is possible to use your scars as a reminder of God's grace rather than the pain. Do you feel at peace with your scars? Do you want to hide them? Do you live a guilt-ridden life? Do you have a grudge against those who have hurt you? Have you experienced bitterness as a result of what you have been through? You don't have to be depressed or discouraged because of those scars. The purpose of their presence is to encourage you. The most important thing about them, though, is that they remind you of what God has brought you through.

There might have been pain involved, or it might not have been fair. In spite of this, you wouldn't be where you are without the goodness of God. You would still be injured and hurting. What a difference God made! You have been restored, healed, and are moving forward. My scars once made me the epitome of bitterness, because I saw the pain I suffered through them every time I looked at them. Thanks to God, now my scars remind me of His faithfulness, because my thinking has been transformed. As a result of my scars, I remember that Almighty God is directing my steps, he has the right people lined up to help me reach my goals. As I look at my scars, I am reminded of the fact that God is for me, regardless of any forces working against me!

It would be great if I could have thirty seconds to talk to myself twenty-nine years ago. My advice to myself would be to renew my mind with God's Word, get in line with God's Word, and remain fixed upon Jesus, the author and perfecter of my faith. Through God's grace, I'm a new creation in Christ Jesus for the first time in my life. My entire life has been transformed by the living Word, Jesus, the Bible, and by the power of the Holy Spirit. It's so great that I no longer have to live a lie. The fact that I am God's son, His workmanship, created in Christ Jesus to do good works, which He prepared in advance for me, makes me so thankful for my salvation.

IT'S NOT ABOUT US

I shrugged off the idea of writing my first book. The first thing I thought to myself was, "Get real!" After a few months, and after being prompted by the Holy Spirit several times, I finally realized it was inspired by God. In spite of the fact that I am just a messenger, I must obey God at all costs, because He is worthy of such obedience. I also realized that God is in control of what happens in my life. My duty, honor, and privilege was not just to obey God, but to serve my fellow man and bear witness to His goodness.

In my former life, it shouldn't have ever been about me, and it shouldn't be today, either. This is all about glorifying God. I almost lost my life due to selfishness and self-centeredness. I experienced hopelessness like you could never imagine at the end of my former life. There is, however, one who has all power, and I have found him now through his son Jesus Christ. Furthermore, I have realized that God has loved me for a very long time before I was ever conceived by my mother.

There is nothing like the love, graciousness, and awesomeness of God. We were created for a relationship with him and with each other. If the enemy of our souls cut me into a million pieces with a paper shredder. It would look like this. You would see a bunch of little hearts that say, "I love Jesus." A bunch of hearts that say, "Jesus loves you." A bunch of hearts that say, "I'm blessed, saved, sanctified, redeemed, justified, and delivered by my Lord and Savior Jesus Christ of Nazareth. Those hearts would tell you, "I am loved, needed, and wanted by the Most High God." This book wasn't written for me, it was written for you. My reason for saying that is because I want you to know that no matter who you are, where you come from, or where you're going, God loves you and that His plan for your life is absolutely more beautiful than you can imagine! It was God's great love for you that He sent His son Jesus Christ to die for you and take the punishment you deserve for your sins. If you accept Jesus Christ as your savior and allow God to take on his rightful place in your heart and life as your savior, you will never regret being a follower of Christ.

GREATEST FEELING ON EARTH

Your search for fulfillment will never be fulfilled in Satan's kingdom. Nevertheless, you will find what you need in God's kingdom, which is his love in Christ Jesus. Our greatest desire is to achieve true happiness, and eternal life, a life rounded out by purpose, joy, peace, and contentment. Brother or sister, isn't it time that you come out of the pain and let God truly be your God? Thank God my life did not end as Satan had planned. As a result of God's touching my heart, I now have a heart of flesh instead of a heart of stone as I once had. Like a body in a grave, I was dead. After everything I had already experienced, there was nothing left of the human being I originally was. I lived in hopelessness and despair that I wouldn't even wish upon Satan.

I used to take trips all over the country and even vacationed in Mexico. There were fine cars, fine women, and fine dining available to me. It was not uncommon for me to wear designer clothing and drive expensive trucks. The country club where I lived was very nice. As a concertgoer, I sat in suites to watch the show. My spending habits were like those of a millionaire. It was my fortune to have three wives and three children. According to world standards, which include power, position, and prestige, I had it all. My dear friend, I have something to share with you. The world can't come close to making me feel like the love of Almighty God in Jesus Christ. If you don't have a relationship with God through Jesus Christ, you are the poorest person on earth. Your bank statement doesn't determine your worth, God does. You must be all you can be in God's Army.

Chapter 7

HUMBLE YOURSELF

A humble heart is a prerequisite to being an effective member of the Army of God. The first sentence of Romans 12:1 says it all, "In view of God's mercy." When you believe you can do nothing for God unless He shows mercy to you, you are on the right path. Romans 12:1 then says, "Offer your body as a living sacrifice, for this is your spiritual act of worship." We must do as Jesus said, for "whoever wants to be my disciple must deny himself and take up his cross every day and follow me." (Luke 9:23, NIV, 2010). Furthermore, you must die to yourself in order to learn that nothing can be done for God except in view of God's mercy, so that you can appreciate his mercy.

This is how I would like you to think about it. The Creator and Sustainer of life doesn't need your worship. It is God who can make the rocks cry out and worship him. In all of creation, God owns everything, and God doesn't need your money. We were created by God as relational beings in his image. Our relationship with God and with each other is based on the relationship he established through his son, Jesus Christ. As the highest order of creation, we are the most important. I only discovered these facts after going through a lot of pain and heartache. In order to worship God properly, you should offer your body as a living sacrifice.

After what Adam and Eve did in the Garden of Eden, it is a generous thing for God to not reward us with what we deserve. It is our sin that condemns us, not God. We are condemned because of our sin problem. Aside from that, God is full of mercy, grace, and love! The reason He sent his son Jesus Christ to die on the cross was so he could give us eternal life, abundant life, and peace with Him. As a result of His love for us, He made us victorious over our sin problem. Every day, the Lord showers His mercies upon us.

My realization over the past few years has been that if I really want to follow Christ, I must be humble, die to myself, and always put myself in a position to serve God and others by being humble. I do this so that God, who is in me working according to his will and good pleasure, can be exalted in my body so that he can accomplish his will through me by way of His Holy Spirit. It is only through humility that I can accomplish this. It is my responsibility to surrender my life to the Lord one day at a time, one moment at a time.

I now fully understand what the great Apostle Paul meant when he stated, "It is not I who lives, but Christ who lives in me and the life I live, I live by faith in the son of God because he loved and gave himself for me" (Galatians 2:20, NIV, 2010). So, my life is not mine alone. The fact that God has given you free will and power of choice does not mean you can waste your life. As we yield to the virtuous promptings of the Holy Spirit, we are obligated to come to an accurate knowledge of the truth so that we may live a life of love and victory before the Lord. The love, grace, and mercy of God have led me to this startling realization. At the end of my previous life, I began to understand what Paul meant in Galatians 2:20 when he said, "Christ loved and gave himself for me." The truth is that Jesus Christ took the punishment for all of our sins. When He died for us so we could receive God's love, grace, and mercy, He got no mercy.

FIGHTING SIN IS FOOLISHNESS

My former life was so bad that I chose to live a lie and serve Satan's purposes over and over again. As I look back, I realize my heart was filled with bitterness, retaliation, anger, hatred, violence, and murder. I lived in absolute darkness for a quarter of a century because of this and the worst thinking on the planet. As a result of choosing to ignore God's Word, I truly believed that was just the way I was and I was powerless to change it.

I'm sure that your first response is probably to think that I realized something was terribly wrong at some point, and you're right. In my case, the problem was how my mind was conditioned. In those days, there were old sayings like "Big boys don't cry," and "A man makes his own way." Like many men, I bought into those lies, trying to stop drinking, partying, and whatever else seemed to make me feel good. In spite of my best efforts, I never enjoyed any success. You cannot fight sin on your own, if we were so good and capable of fighting sin, God would not have sent Jesus to the cross to pay the price for our sins.

I had a spiritual problem/sin problem which was impossible for me to solve on my own, which is why I failed at quitting drinking and partying. The Bible says, 14 "We know that the law is spiritual; but I am unspiritual, sold as a slave to sin. 15 I do not understand what I do. For what I want to do I do not do, but what I hate I do. 16 And if I do what I do not want to do, I agree that the law is good. 17 As it is, it is no longer I myself who does it, but it is sin living in me. 18 For I know that good itself does not dwell in me, that is, in my sinful nature. For I have the desire to do what is good, but I cannot carry it out. 19 For I do not do the good I want to do, but the evil I do not want to do—this I keep on doing. 20 Now if I do what I do not want to do, it is no longer I who do it, but it is sin living in me that does it" (Romans 7:14-20, NIV, 2010).

I want you to understand something I didn't comprehend until almost losing my life. As I got sober, I lost my mother, my aunt, watched two brothers become addicted to heroin and methamphetamine, watched my youngest daughter go through foster care, and watched my father inch towards death while in prison. During my time in prison, I have seen so many addicts die of addiction that it is heartbreaking. I watched my daughters grow up without me, calling another man father.

All this because I never took the time to understand my problem was all of humanity's problem. It was a SIN PROBLEM and the wages of sin is death! I wish I could go back and know what I know now, and live my life all over again and love one woman and my children well as a Godly man, husband, and father. Sadly, we only get one shot at life. My dear friend listen to my voice. There is only one way to defy the Curse of the Law of Sin and Death that was passed down to all of humanity through Adam and Eve and that is to truly understand the Bible where it says, "Because through Christ Jesus the law of the Spirit who gives life has set you free from the law of sin and death" (Romans 8:2, NIV, 2010). I want to make this as simple as possible for you to understand. When we surrender our hearts and lives to the Lord one day at a time, one moment at a time. God by way of his Holy Spirit can be exalted in our bodies to do his will and finish his work. God produces what God requires, which is obedience, which leads to righteousness by way of his Spirit when we die to self, and surrender our God given free will back to him humbly offering our bodies as a living sacrifice, because He is worthy.

We do this by understanding fundamental Bible truth. The Bible says, "'Not by might nor by power, but by my Spirit,' says the Lord Almighty" (Zechariah 4:6, NIV, 2010). There is no way for us to deal with our sin problem unless we acknowledge that we are powerless over it. There is one who has all power, and that is Almighty God, and it is through his son Jesus Christ that we are freed from our sin problem. You will continually attempt to fight sin on your own if you don't know and understand this. Our effort to fight this battle by ourselves is absolutely foolish, since we were never meant to do so. As well, this is a battle we cannot win without the help of Almighty God and his son, Jesus Christ.

CURSE OF THE LAW

I would like to make this more practical for you. Due to the Law of Gravity, if you drop a book in Bay St. Louis, Mississippi, Bangkok, Thailand, or Moscow, Russia, it will fall ten times out of ten. We all know and believe that there is a Law of Gravity, regardless of whether you can see or feel it. The Law of Gravity can be defied by holding my arm straight out with that same book in my hand. There is still a Law of Gravity. Do you think I could hold that book for an hour with my arm straight out? In the end, I would give in to gravity and my arm would give out. That is exactly how we are with our sin.

Whatever our level of resistance to sin, no matter how strong our God-given free will, one day we will succumb to the Curse of the Law of Sin and Death. It was passed down to humanity through Adam and Eve. If I fill a balloon with helium, it will float. As a result, a higher law takes effect. While the Law of Gravity still seeks to pull the balloon down to its grounding, the Law of Buoyancy has already taken effect. The balloon has helium inside, which explains this. In the absence of helium, the balloon would fall due to gravity. Since there is a higher Law of Buoyancy, the balloon will begin to float upwards. The Curse of the Law of Sin and Death also works in exactly the same way, by constantly causing us to sin against God and exalt ourselves above measure. As Christians, when we struggle with sin without Jesus Christ as our savior, we are just like balloons without helium. It might seem that we can beat our sin problem for a few moments, but ultimately we lose the game.

In essence, we are telling God of the universe that he does not have the right to run our lives. Consequently, we stand condemned by our sin problem because of our selfishness. My point is that a higher law can defeat the curse. There is such a law found in the Bible, it says, "Because through Christ Jesus the law of the Spirit who gives life has set you free from the law of sin and death" (Romans 8:2, NIV, 2010). In order to truly comprehend what it means to be a child of God, you must understand what makes you a child of God. According to the Bible, "13 For if you live according to the flesh, you will die; but if by the Spirit you put to death the misdeeds of the body, you will live. 14 For those who are led by the Spirit of God are the children of God. 15 The Spirit you received does not make you slaves, so that you live in fear again; rather, the Spirit you received brought about your adoption to sonship. And by him we cry, "Abba, Father" (Romans 8:13-15, NIV, 2010). As we surrender to God's Spirit, we can be led by the Holy Spirit to carry out God's will in our bodies and accomplish his purpose. When we die to self, God's Spirit can work in our bodies to do God's will in the world.

This is why it is so vital to have your mind renewed with God's word and to understand Bible truth, so you can come to a true understanding of the Word. Conversely, if you don't know the truth, you default to living a lie and living in a defeated victim's mindset. My knowledge of this does not come from someone else who told me about it. My own poor choices and ignorance of God's words led me to live a lie for twenty-nine years of my life. Until you accept that you have a sin problem and that you need a relationship with God through Jesus Christ, you will perpetually exalt yourself above measure. The whole point is foolish pride, and you will tell God in your action, "I believe in you Lord, I even prayed the "Sinner's Prayer", but you don't have the right to run my life, you are not worthy of my obedience." That's absolute foolishness!

UNDERSTANDING THE SPIRITUAL MALADY

You cannot begin to live a successful life until you understand your sin problem, which means that if you don't deal with it, you will live a lie and be defeated before you even start. It is important for you to understand that your success in life is not measured by your portfolio, it comes from your understanding of what God has done for you through Jesus Christ. The wages of sin is death/condemnation (Romans 6:23, NIV, 2010), and if you don't understand this, you will die in your sin. Despite what you may feel, I want you to know that God is not condemning you, it is your sin that has done that. The sad fact is that without believing this, you will always be satisfied with a good life at the most, as opposed to the best life that God can offer you.

It seems that we as a race are constantly filled with pride and exalting ourselves above all else. As a loving, gracious God, the Lord keeps calling us back through the way of humility. The goodness of God motivates him to do this, along with the fact that God opposes the proud, but gives grace to the humble. There is no limit to the mercy and compassion of our God, my dear friend. That took me a lifetime to figure out. As a result of being stripped of everything that life has to offer, and of all that makes it worthwhile, I was finally able to say in humility, after twenty-nine years, "Lord, I acknowledge I'm a sinner. I need Jesus Father. Can you please save me from my sin problem and glorify yourself in and through me? I accept Jesus as my savior." A man like me admitting he has a sin problem takes a lot of humility.

The Bible says, "For *those* who *exalt* themselves *will* be humbled, and *those who humble themselves will be exalted*" (Matthew 23:12, NIV, 2010). Whenever you are clothed in Christ-like humility, then God can be exalted within you, since God is working through you in accordance with His will. The Bible contains about 58 references to pride and over 100 references to humility. As far as sins go, pride is at the top. A further benefit of humility is that it counteracts pride perfectly. As a result of being stripped of my pride, money, houses, cars, and jobs, I discovered that what I was searching for was Christ's love for me and the one and only true God. It was so difficult at times that I wanted to end my life. Ultimately, what stopped me was that I believed in God.

The world was so attractive to me that I just didn't believe God was deserving of my obedience. In the Bible, it says, 4 "You adulterous people, don't you know that friendship with the world means enmity against God? Therefore, anyone who chooses to be a friend of the world becomes an enemy of God. 5 "Or do you think Scripture says without reason that he jealously longs for the spirit he has caused to dwell in us" (James 4:4-5, NIV, 2010). That's exactly what I said to God through my actions for twenty-nine years. Essentially, I said, "I believe in you Lord, but I love the world, myself, and alcohol more." In reality, I said, "I will not submit, you are not worthy enough." The same thing was done long ago in the Garden of Eden by Adam and Eve.

There is something deeply saddening for me in the fact that people from every continent are still doing what I did out of ignorance of the Word of God, saying, "I am the god of my life, I will not submit." I am thankful to God for His patience and for not allowing me to die in my sin. I have watched so many people die senselessly in these last four years without Jesus. There is a deep sadness in my heart to the point of despair. My life has seen more deaths in the last four years than in the previous forty. I'm grateful to be alive.

IT'S WHO I AM

The Hancock County Sheriff's Office's Captain Johnson once asked me, "Why do you do what you do if rehab success rates for people who do drugs are so low?" I answered, "I don't do this, it's who I am. I am a child of the living God, a messenger of the Lord, I help people who are hopeless, fallen people." Instantly, I could envision the faces of addicts who lost the fight and died. My eyes filled with tears as I said, "There is a living hope, and that hope is Jesus. He is our only hope." I am saying "That Jesus is your only hope, your only true unconditional hope."

If you put your trust in Jesus, you can live a full and happy life. The scriptures say, "Here I am! I stand at the door and knock. If you hear my voice and open the door I will open the door, I will come in and eat with you, and you will eat with me" (Revelation 3:20, NIV, 2010). Do you feel that Jesus is knocking at the door of your heart? Yet you refuse to answer because something or someone else is more important to you than God? You are forgiven by God, answer the door, and let the son of God into your heart.

I remember standing by a swimming pool watching a friend of mine swim around in the summer of 1986. I was pushed into the water by another young man coming up behind me. My inability to swim was unknown to anyone! As I was drowning at the bottom of the pool, a friend of mine came to my aid after what seemed like an eternity. Suddenly, I felt a hand grab mine, and I pushed myself to the surface. As soon as I surfaced, I took a big breath of fresh air. It was a great feeling to be alive.

It was in 2018 that I came to the point of true repentance, which led to salvation without regret. After almost drowning back in

1986, I felt like I did when I took my first breath of fresh air. The realization that I would be dead if it weren't for God's grace made me appreciate life just as much. I've realized now how close to death I was due to my sin problem not being addressed by Jesus. The sin problem also destroyed every relationship I ever had, and my self-destructive behavior eventually relegated me to a hell of self-inflicted tortures. An unknown force stopped me just before I crashed into eternity and gave me the choice to accept his grace through his son Jesus Christ.

LIVED TO TELL THE TALE

I often think to myself, "Wow, now that is living on the edge!" I often think, "You fool, you almost killed yourself." I am making light of a very painful and serious situation that God allowed me to overcome through his grace. However, I have also seen numerous people die in their sin problem, their spiritual malady. It is so tragic that so many people did not live to tell the tale. My relationship with God has been made possible by His son Jesus Christ, and I am so grateful to him for it. It is amazing to receive God's love through Jesus Christ because He is exalted in our bodies through the Holy Spirit by the way we surrender our lives and hearts to him. In light of this, it is Christ rather than I who lives. The fruits of the Spirit begin to manifest in my life and God begins to grow us toward our God-given purpose.

We maintain healthy relationships because we are made in the image of Almighty God, which has a profound effect on how we relate to each other. This also helps us realize that people are not the real enemy, but Satan. As a result of the fact that God is in us, we can love people as God first loved us through Jesus Christ. There is more significance to who a person is than what they do, based on who they are, God's creation. As a result, we are humbled and are able to see we all have a sin problem, and we need Jesus Christ to liberate us from the bonds of sin and self. When God shows up through Christ Jesus, His one and only son in humanity, that is what

He does. There are those who claim they cannot see God. I can't accept that because I see Him everywhere around me. It is the fact that I know him personally that makes the difference. I would like to ask you a question: Do you know God personally? Do you see the wind blow? The answer to that is no, but it is there. So is God!

BEING THE CHANGE

It's funny how life works out sometimes. My life was perfect by the world's standards, and then I lost it all. The road I was on was a search for significance. It just hadn't occurred to me at the time. I lived in the oh poor, pitiful, defeated state that we are all born with, which drives us towards the bondage of self and sin. The thought of looking back on my former life now is kind of crazy because I've changed so much. My circumstances and situations used to be a source of blame for my wrongdoings, and I would blame everyone else. Throughout my life I have waited for people, places, and things in this world to change. Unfortunately, that line of thinking does not work. In the beginning, when I began studying the Bible to renew my mind. I realized the things that were happening to me are now happening for me instead.

According to one of my favorite Bible verses, "All things work together for good, to those who love the Lord, and are called according to his purpose" (Romans 8:28, NIV, 2010). My eyes were opened to the fact that it was time to take on Christ's humility, humbling myself to the point of death, and dying to myself one day at a time. My realization was that now was the time to start being the change that I wanted to see in the world, and in the people, places, and things around me. It was at that moment when I realized I would offer my body to God every day, and then to my fellow man. It would now be my pleasure to serve Almighty God after serving Satan for the past twenty-nine years.

It was then that I decided to pursue my God-given destiny, which is greatness, for His glory. In this shocking revelation, it comes as no surprise that those to whom much is given, much is required, as the good Lord spared my life from an imminent overdose of heroin. I had literally been made a modern-day miracle by God. A life of abundance, joy, peace, and true freedom in my heart, mind, and soul has been bestowed upon me by God. As a result of God setting me free, I was able to forget what is behind and press forward toward the goal, for the high calling of God in Christ Jesus. My life was transformed by His amazing grace through the sacrifice of His son, Jesus Christ. I realized that it was God's grace that enabled me to change, so that I was now able to assist others in changing. My greatest honor is being able to help others.

It became my mission to help others no matter what it takes. My mission was to proclaim liberty to captives and call out to those in darkness, "Come out of the darkness." In this vision, I see how those who humble themselves will be exalted, while those who exalt themselves will be humbled. I am living proof of that in both my past and present lives. As a result, when I humble myself to the point of death, I die to myself one day at a time. Then, God, who is acting in me according to his will and good pleasure, will be exalted in my body to accomplish His will and complete His work. This results in him glorifying himself through me.

He does all this through the power of his Holy Spirit. I must remain humble in order to truly surrender my life to the Lord, so he can use me to help others. It is important for me to align myself with what God's Word says about me and others and never stop praying for His will to be done on earth, in my life, and in other people's lives. In truth, none of this is possible without me being humble and keeping my mind fixed on the Lord. The reality is that God can accomplish in a blink of an eye what you and I couldn't do on our best day in a thousand lifetimes!

LUKEWARM CHRISTIANS

The Bible, however, is the only way to bring true transformation from the inside out since it is what renews the mind through Scripture. You can only truly walk by faith if you renew your mind through the Word of God. It also teaches you how to walk humbly through this life one day at a time through obedience to God's Word. It was early in my walk with the Lord when I realized that the only difference between carnally minded Christians and absolute surrendered, 100% committed followers of Christ was that the followers of Christ had undergone true transformation through the Word of God. Those who are carnally minded have nothing because they are lukewarm. According to the Bible, "So, because you are lukewarm—neither hot nor cold—I am about to spit you out of my mouth" (Revelation 3:16, NIV, 2010). According to that verse, Jesus describes the church at Laodicea as lukewarm. The ancient people drank hot or cold beverages at feasts and in religious sacrifices, but never lukewarm ones. Those liquids are unattractive, and for good reason: they are more likely to harbor bacteria. A cold drink is refreshing on a hot day, and a hot drink is energizing on a cold day, but a lukewarm drink is never enjoyed.

Laodicea lacked its own source of water. It drew its water from Hierapolis, a nearby city. Through an aqueduct, Hierapolis provided Laodicea with abundant hot water from a number of hot springs. In Laodicea, however, the water was lukewarm after cooling to a lukewarm temperature on its way. Prior to consumption, it would need to be cooled or re-heated. It made Jesus feel sick that the Laodiceans' religious life was lukewarm, to the point of making Him feel like vomiting the church up.

It also provides a useful analogy for evangelism. People who are spiritually "hot" are actively involved in their faith. It is possible for people who are "cold" to be impacted by the gospel in a powerful way. Those who are merely "lukewarm" are actually in a worse condition than those who are "cold." Their knowledge of Jesus is limited, so they are not resistant, but they are also somewhat calloused to His voice. In Jesus' opinion, it is better to be spiritually "cold" since it means you're more likely to recognize God's call.

In general, people who are carnally minded Christians have faith that serves their purposes and they treat God as a genie in a bottle that serves their purposes. Therefore, that person is still deceived and still setting themselves up as god of their lives, saying,

"God, I believe in you, but you don't deserve to be glorified with my life. Therefore, I will do what I want to, not what you want me to do." The carnally minded Christian is actually saying, "God, I want to do my will, not yours." This is pride at its finest and pride is self-exaltation. It is an abomination to God to be prideful, and God gives grace to the humble whereas the proud are opposed by God.

The true disciple of Christ wakes up every morning asking God who and what his or her assignment is for the day. Furthermore, they know that they are God's friends because Jesus made us his friends. Jesus also set the example for the true follower of Christ by saying, "Greater love has no one than this: to lay down one's life for one's friends" (John 15:13, NIV, 2010). While we were still sinners, Christ died for us. As His followers, we can follow his example and find joy, peace, and contentment in life. When we help others, we find joy, peace, and contentment as true disciples of Christ.

One of the amazing things about Jesus was that He did not consider Himself equal to God. The cross was the point at which he humbled himself to the point of death. Those who follow Christ should live by the example God set through Christ. It is true that I am God's friend, but I am also his slave. Since I am a Christ'-follower, I do this because it is not I who live, but Christ in me. I surrender my life to the Lord daily as I watch Him work through me, by the power of the Holy Spirit, and take part in loving and helping his fallen creation.

BATTLE BELONGS TO THE LORD

My life can only be surrendered to the Lord when I am clothed in humility. When I first learned these principles, I realized that whenever I surrender my God-given free will and my life to the Lord, I am allowing God to work in and through me to help others. It fills me with great joy because so many hopeless people need God's help so desperately in this cruel, evil, Satan-controlled world. There is no doubt that Satan holds the upper hand in this cold and cruel world. The good thing is that in all of creation, God remains a sovereign Lord in control of all things. Despite living in an evil world, I don't believe Almighty God has ever called an emergency meeting. It is because God knows, what the true follower of Christ knows, that the battle belongs to the Lord!

It was Jesus Christ of Nazareth who defeated sin, sickness, disease, death, and Satan's kingdom. All of that was accomplished by God through the death, burial, resurrection, and ascension of Jesus Christ. The Bible says, 24 "But because Jesus lives forever, he has a permanent priesthood. 25 Therefore he is able to completely save those who come to God through him, because he always lives to intercede for them. 26 Such a high priest truly meets our need—one who is holy, blameless, pure, set apart from sinners, exalted above the heavens" (Hebrews 7:24-26, NIV, 2010). My realization that the battle belongs to the Lord took almost thirty years. It was Jesus who gave us the victory on the cross. Death, oh death, where is your sting? We believe in the resurrection of Jesus the Messiah. It is Jesus who holds the keys to the gates of Hell!

The great deceiver, Satan himself, will be cast into Hell by Jesus one day. The realization that God is all-powerful gave me great hope. It helped me realize that He who is in me is greater than he who is in the world. As another way of putting it, the forces that are on my side and your side are greater than anything that can harm us. God is for us, so there is nothing that can stand against us! My bondage to sin and self was liberated by these simple biblical truths. It would have been great if I had applied these simple truths to my life twenty-nine years ago. There were a lot more people who could have been helped by me. The people I hurt by my actions would have been considerably fewer as a result. The greatest tragedy in human history is our choice not to know God's Word.

My situation is unique in that God turned what was meant to destroy me into something that helped me. I was given beauty for ashes by God. I was left with nothing but ashes after I had finished living my former life. It is the absolute truth that God, who is rich in mercy, continually reached out to me with patience, kindness, care, and compassion. I'm so thankful for God's love, grace, and mercy that kept on coming to me. I can say with certainty that God kept calling me back through humility.

Throughout my life, God allowed me to be stripped of everything that made life worthwhile. The reason God did this was so I would see that what I really needed was the love of God through Christ Jesus. My true desire was to have a relationship with God through Jesus Christ. I was created and designed by God to serve his purposes, and I realized that at the end of the day. This is all achieved through humility. When you are not humble, you default to pride, and God opposes the proud, but gives grace to the humble. Remember that God is able to do for you what you are unable to do for yourself. The way of humility leads to all of this. The only way to receive God's grace is through Jesus Christ and humility.

Chapter 8

GRACE

I was incarcerated at the Hancock County Jail in Bay St. Louis, Mississippi on a cold October day. As I got down on my knees in a cold dark cell, in my pod, I remember it like it was yesterday. It was bitterly cold inside the pod, like a freezer. The hopelessness of my life seemed so overwhelming to me at that time. The more I reflect on my life now, the more I realize how hopelessness and despair had become the norm in my life. In order for me to make it back to where I belong in humanity, I required the grace of God. My past dominated my present. An unseen enemy had been slaughtering me for 29 years. Through the riches of this world and my constant memories of the pains of the past, Satan made sure that I was rendered useless to the Kingdom of God. In order to keep me living in the past, Satan used two different distractors.

The worst enemy I sometimes faced was myself. The outside of my body was covered in scars, but the inside was covered in a mountain of these scars. The pain was too much for me to bear and the weight of the world was too heavy for me to carry. I couldn't move one step further because the burden was too heavy for me to carry alone. It was impossible for me to continue living as I did. That's when I realized I no longer had any fight left in me. It was at that moment that I realized that I would rather die than to continue living the way I was!

In my mind, I considered death to be a better option than my current situation. There was nothing worse than being sick and tired. There was something that needed to be changed at that moment. At the time, I didn't realize that I was suffering a mental breakdown.

In my mind, I remember thinking, "This is over!" My soul collapsed as I pleaded with God to take this burden and self-induced torture from me and provide me with a new life.

There was a need for me to be released from my self-imposed prison. There was nothing I knew about freedom, all I knew was slavery. It had never occurred to me to learn how to be free. My only recourse was to fight on with my God-given free will until the bitter end. My experience in the world taught me how to fight. I was never taught how to surrender my free will to God through Jesus Christ, and the way of humility. There was something I wanted to do differently, but I didn't know how.

As a result of not knowing Jesus, I was as dead as a man in the grave. All I knew was myself as god! It took me a long time to realize that I needed God's grace. There was no doubt in my mind that grace and Jesus Christ were what I needed! The grace of God is found in Jesus Christ, and Christ is the gift of mercy from God. It was almost as if my faith was absent, I read the following verse: "The law was given through Moses, but grace and truth came through Jesus Christ" (John 1:17, NIV, 2010).

Suddenly, I remembered a verse I learned as a child. It was almost as if something in my spirit whispered in my ear, 7 "Ask and it will be given to you; seek and you will find; knock and the door will be opened to you. 8 For everyone who asks receives; the one who seeks finds; and to the one who knocks, the door will be opened" (Matthew 7:7-8, NIV, 2010). It was then that I said, "God, I take full responsibility for everything I have done. In effect, I was saying, "God, please help me, I do not want to be like this anymore." In retrospect, when I got up off the floor, I felt like I was no longer alone for the first time in my life. There was a sense that I had been relieved of my burdens by someone. Jesus said, 28 "Come to me, all you who are weary and burdened, and I will give you rest. 29 Take my yoke upon you and learn from me, for I am gentle and humble in heart, and you will find rest for your souls. 30 For my yoke is easy and my burden is light" (Matthew 11:28-30, NIV, 2010). I can attest to the truth of that statement found in the scriptures. I'm thankful that God was able to accomplish in the blink of an eye what I couldn't accomplish for myself in the twenty-nine years of my former life. It was the first time in my life, I relinquished my free will and my life back to God, the Creator and Sustainer of all life.

HOW GOD REVEALED HIMSELF

My survival was solely due to God's amazing saving and sustaining grace. My study of the Bible intensified and I attended numerous meetings of Alcoholics Anonymous. As a way of serving others, I helped set up chairs before meetings and pour coffee for inmates at meetings. Often, I was under the watchful eye of my mentor and good friend, Chaplain Dan Munger. I'm almost certain I watched his actions closer than he watched mine. It used to be a constant sight for me to watch Dan and Joan Munger entering the Hancock County Jail day after day. My eyes were captivated by these two gorgeous, bright shining examples of the love of God in Christ Jesus. The inmates inside the Hancock County Jail, as well as many people on the outside, have benefited greatly from their time, talents, works, and possessions. Their smiles were always contagious. It was always a pleasure to hear them speak kind words about others. There was never any complaint from them. God was showing me that the joy of the Lord is our strength at the time, but I did not realize it.

In fact, Dan often got up as early as me, at seventy years old, and I often woke up at two in the morning. God also revealed to me that Dan and Joan received God's saving grace through his son, Jesus Christ. It was easy to see them love God in truth and in action every single day. As I watched them, I witnessed God's goodness and saving grace at work in humanity. As a result of my spiritual eyes being opened, I saw that Dan and Joan Munger were acting according to God's good pleasure. These two genuine Christians were God's instruments of righteousness.

It was because of this that not only my life and eternal destiny was altered, but also the lives and eternal destiny of countless other people. It should be noted, however, that Dan Munger and Joan

Munger would never take any credit for anything they accomplished. My love for them and my love for God grew even deeper because I saw Christ in them. I consider these two individuals to be my earthly heroes. They believed in me even when I did not believe in myself at my darkest hour. After receiving God's grace and having my mind renewed by the word of God, I know. Joan, Dan, and I all have the same hero. There is one name above all names: Jesus Christ of Nazareth.

The more I studied God's Word and came to understand his nature, the more I fell in love with Him. As a result of receiving God's grace, my spiritual eyes were certainly opened. My eyes were suddenly opened to the valiant work of God in Dan and Joan's lives. I could see him working in humanity in accordance with his will. I was astonished by what I saw. These two gentle souls had more love in their little finger for people than all of the love in humanity. My salvation was worked out with trembling and fear as I made my way toward my God-given destiny.

My life was handed over to the Lord one moment at a time, one day at a time. God is so merciful and kept giving me grace in all that I said, thought, and did so that I could carry out His will and accomplish His purposes. I have made a lot of mistakes on my journey, so I'm almost certain God has a sense of humor. I am thankful that God was as patient with me as a mother is with her child when it comes to learning how to walk. There is only one love, and that is God! I thank God for His love and mercy through Dan and Joan Munger.

TRUST IN THE LORD

While I was walking by faith, I experienced some devastating circumstances, but God never failed me. In 2020, my mother died, and the void that her death created within me nearly killed me. About a month after my mother's death, her sister, my aunt, passed away. An older brother of mine was diagnosed with liver cancer. A priest read the last rites for my older brother, who was in a medically induced coma at the time. As of right now, my brother is still alive. The doctors drained the fluid off his abdomen, then took the tube out of his stomach a week later after he woke up. When he exited the hospital against doctors' orders, he was on two cains, and he immediately began using heroin again! It's not my intention to sponsor such behavior, but he deserves it. He's stronger than any team in the NFL! Sadly, my younger brother became addicted to methamphetamine. My youngest daughter went into foster care while I was in prison. I experienced all of this while faithfully serving the Lord. I just kept on showing up and trusting in the Lord with all my heart. That is exactly what the Bible teaches us to do. A lot of people witnessed these things and it glorified God.

The fact that I was teaching two Bible classes in addition to an in-house rehab and helping the volunteer chaplains when they got locked out of the building was by the grace of God. I was also working sixteen hours a day at the Hancock County Jail. Every single day, I ate, slept, and breathed the right thing. There were people dying all around me; it was absolutely horrific. I saw a young lady I knew leaving Hancock County Jail one day as I walked down the hall. After she was released from jail, this young lady overdosed on fentanyl and died five hours later. Ironically, I can still see her face and hear her say, "Take care of yourself Odell." This is such a tragedy.

BY THE GRACE OF GOD

One day I was getting ready for class in the back classroom of the jail, just as I had done so many times before. This time, however, was different. The sign was posted near the ceiling as I looked up. There was a small message that read, "But for the grace of God." That was all there was to it! I had survived things that other people had died for, and I had survived things that others had died for but did a great deal less than me. I had been shot at, my mother had died, my aunt had died, my children had been raised without their father, and I had been in prison three times. In prison, I was housed with some of the world's most violent criminals, some of them murderers. My good fortune was that, by the grace of God, I came out of it all alive. The absolute truth is that God's grace is more promiscuous than I was with women in my former life. While I was going through all this, I kept saying, "God helped me get through this, and I may weep for an evening, but joy will follow in the morning." A lot of catastrophic circumstances were taking place in my life, and to top it all off, I faced 56 mandatory years in prison. Even though I was down at the moment, I wasn't dead. As I stood helplessly and watched, I kept telling myself "This too shall pass." Through Jesus Christ, I had discovered a living hope after being hopeless for so long. I urge you, my dear friend, to listen to my voice; the answer is Jesus!

Through God's grace, I now have a heart of flesh instead of a heart of stone. I once was unable to give or receive love, but now through God's amazing grace and faith, I have received God's love and can love the unlovable. I used to only see my problems, but now thanks to the grace of God, I know the solution to all my troubles and those of the whole world! In the past, I was part of the problem; now, by God's grace, I am part of the solution to my problems and the problems of the world. Through the grace of God, I can now see clearly from a biblical perspective and have an accurate perception of life. My dear friend, I once walked in absolute darkness, but thanks to God's grace, today I know Jesus Christ to be the light of the world.

COUNT IT ALL JOY

After being shown humility, through the example of Jesus Christ, it took me a seemingly endless period of time to receive God's saving grace. After making my good profession of faith, I came to a startling realization before it was all over: I had to keep my eyes forever fixed on Jesus. This was necessary to continue receiving God's grace on a daily basis. It was necessary to do this in order to survive this trial by fire we call life. It took me about four years to learn how to count it all joy, and I had to do so regardless of what happened.

I learned one of the most important fundamental truths about the Bible early on in my walk with the Lord. It is the good Lord who gives and the good Lord who takes, but blessed be the name of the Lord God Almighty. Whenever we go through whatever we're going through, God's mercy will give us the grace to get through it, and for that reason, God deserves all the praise, glory, and honor in my life. A burden that is too much for us will never be placed upon us by God. We are able to do everything we need to do through Christ, who strengthens us, because God gives us the ability to receive his love, grace, and mercy through Christ, which enables us to do what we need to do through humility. It is precisely for this reason that the true follower of Christ can overcome just about anything by faith in the Lord. It is God's saving and sustaining grace in Jesus Christ that allows that to be possible.

"In 1965 the country of Romania was occupied by communist. They brutally tortured Christians. They would start to brutally beat the Christian's at their feet. This torture would slowly wind up towards their head. It was an absolutely horrific experience. The communist would then nurse the prisoner back to health and start all over again. All of this because they were Christian's in a communist country. Several of the tortured Christians made it to the United States. One of the prisoner's eventually became a minister in the United States. He told of his horrific experience with his communist torturer's.

Then after fourteen years, the communist decided to release him to go to the United States. Someone had paid a ransom for him to be released. They warned him not to say anything about his experience or communist torturer's. The amazing thing about the minister's release is before he departed from Romania, he went to the Colonel's grave that ordered his arrest and torture for fourteen years. The minister placed a flower on the Colonel's grave. He later thanked God for his grace to get through the tragic ordeal, and said "I hate communism, but I love the men, because they are God's creation." He later went on to say, "They can kill the Christian, but they can't kill the love of God in Christ Jesus that lives in them" (Wurmbrand, 1967).

There is something I would like to promise you. It doesn't matter who you are or where you come from. A relationship with God and receiving his grace can be achieved if you are humble, surrender your free will and every detail of your life to him one moment at a time, one day at a time. Here are a few questions I want to ask you. When was the last time you said "God, let your will be done in my life?" When was the last time you said "God, you are worthy of glory, honor, and praise in my life and all of creation?" When was the last time the God of the universe really took his rightful place in your life? Perhaps He has, maybe He hasn't, or maybe once He did, but you have replaced God with something else. Let me encourage you right now to be humble and accept God's grace. There is no limit to God's ability!

YOUR A MASTERPIECE

The apple of God's eye is you. The Lord sees you as unique, special, and irreplaceable. In all of creation, no one has your DNA, and Almighty God broke the mold when He created you. All the hairs on your head are counted by God. You are loved so much that the Lord gives you the freedom to do whatever you want with your life, including wasting it the way I did. I lived a good life previous to my current one, and you can do the same. Unfortunately, good is the product of mediocrity. As compared with your God-given destiny, which is greatness! Compared to the great life that God has in store for you, a good life is settling for less.

In my former life, I made and squandered a lot of money. Sadly, money wouldn't get rid of my problem's, it complicated them. A Jewish Proverb says, "If you have problems that money can fix, you have no problems at all." I almost lost my life, trying to find what you're searching for and that is true life, true happiness, abundant life, eternal life, a life of meaning, joy, peace, and contentment, crowned with a sense of purpose and favor from the Most High God. There is a God that loves you so much that He sent his son to die in your place. Jesus Christ took the punishment you and I rightfully deserved for our sins. He did this so that we can live a life of victory to God's glory. This is what you need and seek. It is my sincere hope that the Living God and Creator of all things would have mercy on you and allow you to receive his grace so that you can possess those things. You can't buy those things; they are a free gift from God.

BREATHING AND BELIEVING

It was a hot summer day at the Hancock County Jail in South Mississippi. It was 2021, and I remember it like it was yesterday. There was ninety percent humidity, and the heat index was well over one hundred degrees. After eight hours of weed eating around the jail, I decided to rest. It was one of those scorching summer days you feel like you're going to die! The back dock of the jail was lined with barbed wire and I was looking up at it. As I gaze at it, the sun glistens off of it and my eyes are wide open, but I am five hundred miles away in Fort Worth, Texas. My third wife and youngest daughter are with me, and I haven't seen them for a long time. Suddenly, reality slapped me in the face.

The thoughts in my head are racing a million miles an hour. The health of my dad isn't good. I am very worried about him. One of my oldest siblings is on his way out of this world and into the world that lies beyond. It would be nice if I could just say goodbye to my brother and father, but I tell myself, "There will be no final goodbyes." I think about my mother. Since my mother passed away a year ago, I feel as if I'm sinking into an abyss of darkness faster than the Titanic. I have lost sight of Jesus and have begun sinking faster than Simon Peter did when he walked on water, doing the supernatural in a natural state, because his eyes were fixed on Jesus.

My mind snaps back to reality and I tell myself to stop playing games and get back to work. There are three hours of work to be done and a class to teach in two hours. A still, small voice whispers to me as I walk inside the building, saying to me, "Son, I understand you feel alone, but you don't get moved by what you feel, what you see, but by what you believe." Son, my word says, "Though my mother and father abandon me, the Lord will receive me" (Psalm 27:10, NIV, 2010).

I turn the corner and see Sheriff Ricky Adam standing there. On the outside I was smiling, but on the inside I was falling apart. He looked at me and asked, "How are you doing, Mr. O'Dell?" I smiled and replied, "I'm breathing and believing. It's a good day to be alive, sir." The day had been challenging for me. In a way, it almost seemed bittersweet. The grace of God had been poured out on me. I had reached my eternal home. It was a sad reality for me to have lost everything that made life worthwhile.

While I wasn't aware of it at the time, God was teaching me what matters most. Our relationship with him and others is based on that. After that, I thought to myself, hold on a minute. The fight isn't over yet. Everything in the universe was created by my Father, the living God. I was promised beauty for ashes by God. It has been a blessing to receive his grace, and for that I am grateful.

I then finished three hours of work in two hours and fifteen minutes. As I entered classroom A107, I set up the room for class, turned on the coffee maker, prayed, and then I went and gathered seven inmates for Chainbreakers' in-house drug rehab. It was a two-and-a-half hour class. When I collapsed into my bed after nineteen hours of work, I was thinking that I had done all I could to help God's creation, to God's glory. The grace of God is beyond comprehension. As I lay in bed that night, I thought about the day I surrendered my life to Jesus and received the grace of God. My circumstances, trials, tribulations, afflictions, distresses, and tumults humbled me before God. When I surrendered my life to the Lord, on that day thirty months earlier, as I stood up from my knees in my cell, I thought about being a new creation in Christ Jesus because I had received God's saving grace through Jesus Christ. It was the first time in my life that I felt at peace and now I was helping others be at peace with God.

In the end, it was only because I had clothed myself in Christ-like humility and died to myself that I was able to achieve this. In that moment, I was thankful for the grace of God through Jesus Christ and the way of humility, as well as that God's grace was continuously providing me with strength to get through a tough time. In addition, I realized that my conversion to Christianity was solely by God's grace. Although I wasn't perfect, I knew a man named Jesus Christ who died thousands of years earlier and took the punishment for my sins. My spirit was filled with love, grace, mercy, strength, and hope like I had never known before. In every moment of my life since that day in my cell when I met Christ, I have experienced something when I looked at God's creation. The eternal destination of my fellow man was always of concern to me.

It is incomprehensible how much grace God has shown us. It is clear to me that God wants a relationship with all of us through His son. It is my belief that only Jesus is the way, the truth, and the life. In my former life, I was indignant, driven by fear, pride, ego, self-delusion, and my indignation. My fear of poverty had driven me to the edge of insanity, and had put me on a collision course with everyone and everything I had ever known. This made me an enemy of God and a friend of Satan. It was there, in the end, where I could see Satan, my god whom I served faithfully for twenty-nine years, waiting to drag me through the gates of Hell, from my own living hell! One of the startling truths is that somewhere along the road to Hancock County. The loving gracious God that I know today fought valiantly for me. As a result, God spared me the imminent death that I had wished for. It was hopeless to believe in self-righteousness any longer. It was only the things of this world that gave me hope in my former life, but at the end of the day they proved to be utterly hopeless.

DIVINE INTERVENTION AND HOPE

A divine intervention had taken place and my Lord and Savior Jesus Christ had appeared. It was almost as if Jesus had shown up right on time and said, "Not this one Satan." Further, I felt as if Jesus had picked me up off the floor after I had just withdrawn from heroin and blown the doors off of my heart with the love of Almighty

God. As a result of his love, I have been able to grow and develop spiritually on a daily basis. This allowed me to take my rightful place in creation. This was all so that the living God could help others through me, one day at a time.

My life still looked like it was in utter ruins, but I realized there was still hope. The good Lord had not brought me this far to leave me hanging. My disappointments, bad breaks, and the people who did me wrong are not the end of the story. God promised us beauty in exchange for ashes. Don't believe the lies that the enemy whispers to you and me about giving up on dreams and settling where we are. The setbacks are preparing us for our destiny at a higher level. In spite of our mistakes, God is still merciful to us. Our loving, gracious, and merciful God still helps us. God will repay you for the years your enemy has stolen from you. Those years you were lonely, sad, sick, and depressed. The good Lord is your vindicator.

The only thing that you need to do is submit to God by being humble through Christ Jesus. It is only through humility that you can receive God's grace. You may be like me and have made many mistakes. There is no better person to trust than our loving, merciful, and gracious God. It may seem impossible, but God has all power. There are things in life that aren't right. God knows about those things. In the same way that God gave me His grace, He will also give you His grace so that you can make it through whatever you're facing. Grace is God's "unmerited favor." By definition, we cannot earn it. The gift of salvation through Jesus Christ is free of charge. When you accept Jesus Christ as your savior, His Holy Spirit is then in you, acting according to His will, and you are able to do all things through Christ who strengthens you. Then you will realize that Jesus Christ is God's gift of love, grace, and mercy to humanity, enabling us to fulfill His will and accomplish His purpose. There is no limit to what the God of all creation can do, my brother or sister.

INSTRUMENT OF HIS RIGHTEOUSNESS

It is an honor for me to be used by the Creator of the universe as an instrument of His righteousness in writing my first two books.

It is truly an honor for me to be able to do this. My accomplishments are a true gift from God, and I am thankful for His grace. You have only been encouraged and thrust towards your God-given destiny by His grace. The Bible says, "For I know the plans I have for you," declares the Lord, "plans to prosper you and not to harm you, plans to give you hope and a future" (Jeremiah 29:11, NIV, 2010).

On this journey of life, I learned a secret. This is something you should never forget. The grace of God is all you have in this world, and without it you will be doomed to an unchecked sin problem that will kill you! The wages of sin is death, but the gift of God is eternal life in Christ Jesus our Lord (Romans 6:23, NIV, 2010). My friend, we all have sinned and fallen short of God's glory (Romans 3:23, NIV,2010). According to the Lord God Almighty, who is the Creator and Sustainer of life, that is the absolute truth.

A great apostle, Paul, wrote thirteen of the twenty-seven books in the New Testament, and he used grace more than anyone else (100 out of 155 times that it is used). In Ephesians 2:4-10 he made explicit what has been said above: "God's mercy is great, and he loved us very much" (2:4), "You have been saved by God's grace" (2:5). "I mean that you have been saved by grace through faith. You did not save yourselves; it was a gift from God" (2:8). Grace means that God's blessing in our lives is his initiative rather than ours, that God's mercy and love is bountiful, and that forgiveness and being saved from sin and its punishment are God's free gift. According to the Bible, it says that God's gift of forgiveness "Was not the result of our own efforts, so you cannot brag about it" (Ephesians 2:9, NIV, 2010). The definition of grace is that it is not earned or deserved, but given to us.

GOD'S POWER IN WEAKNESS

As I told you earlier, I was once the king of pride. I have destroyed every relationship I have ever had because of my pride, and pride will destroy you too! There is something about our human pride toward God that causes us to misinterpret God's gift of grace as the natural state of our own efforts and abilities (James 4:6, NIV,2010). The greatest story I have ever heard outside of the cross and the Christ is the story of the prodigal son in Luke 15, where the older brother represents our rational resistance to God's forgiveness. A story like the prodigal son shocks us to realize how amazing God's grace is. The Apostle Paul notes this same attitude in Ephesians 2:8-9 and Philippians 3:4-7, and describes a personal lesson he learned through a "painful physical problem" (2 Corinthians 12:7). Paul asked God to take away his physical problem three times. On the third time God answered from the heavens and said, "My grace is sufficient for you, for my power is made perfect in weakness. Therefore I will boast all the more gladly about my weaknesses, so that Christ's power may rest on me."

The point of God's message was that "when you are weak, then you are strong, my power is made perfect in you." It is in our helplessness that we often learn God's gracious gift of love, strength, and mercy. In humility, by reaching out to God, and by admitting need, those who desire and need God's strength find it best. This important lesson about God's grace gave the Apostle Paul a clear and persistent weakness. My lifetime of bad choices and pain led me to realize that we can never earn God's forgiveness, which is found only through knowing Jesus Christ as Lord. I almost died at age forty-one when I realized that those who know God's salvation from sin and its punishment know that it is based on God's kindness in Christ: "By God's grace, he died for everyone" (Hebrews 2:9, NIV, 2010).

I finished reading the Bible cover-to-cover for the first time in 2019. It is no coincidence that the Bible ends with this beautiful, rich blessing, "The grace of our Lord Jesus be with all. Amen" (Revelation 22:21, NIV, 2010). It is impossible for a human mind to comprehend God's grace. I was standing outside one day in Bay St. Louis, Mississippi, on a hot, sunny day. The inmates' families were leaving the visitation area on a Saturday, and I was on the back dock. It was impossible not to notice the wives, mothers, fathers, and children there. My compassion for the families of the inmates moved me at that moment. I realized that they too had suffered from their loved ones being in prison. Their children were growing up without a father due to his incarceration.

Although these wives raised their children to the best of their abilities, they are not able to be both mothers and fathers. As I prayed briefly for the inmates and their families, I felt the presence of God. We were both right there at that moment, just God and I. Afterward, God told me, "I've provided them with love, grace, and mercy to help them get through it. Just as I've given you my love, grace, and mercy for this son." I smiled as I shook my head and thought as I looked up at the blazing sun with a pair of dark sunglasses on. It never ceases to amaze me, God, how awesome you are. After that, God spoke to me in a still, small voice in my spirit, saying "I have supplied your needs according to my riches and glory in Christ Jesus. All you need is my grace, you have it." Wow, God is awesome! In all my years serving the Lord, there has never been a single day that I have regretted it.

Chapter 9

STRIPPED

In Arlington, Texas, it was a hot and sunny day. My friends and I were playing football outside. I was twelve years old at the time. A few months later, my father gave me my first drink of alcohol behind a convenience store. My first experience with illicit drugs was cocaine a few weeks later! As a result of my first drink, I started stealing cars and breaking into houses with my older friends within two months. It wasn't long before I went from making A's and B's in school, to not even attending school at all. I was going down in a blaze of glory and was in a tailspin that was unrecoverable. While I was unaware of it at the time, my glory lay in my shame, my destiny was destruction, and my god would soon be myself, pride, and Satan, the father of lies and pride. My so-called friends and I got busted about four months into our little car theft ring. As a result, I was sent to Central Texas, from North Texas. In those days, it was a small town with about three thousand residents. It was the town of Burnett, Texas.

There were approximately 150 children on the boys ranch. There were some children there who were in foster care. Most of them were sent there as punishment by the juvenile court system for getting into trouble with the law. The latter part of that applies to me. There was a structured environment at the boys ranch, and we were required to attend church. We attended the First Baptist Church of Kingsland, Texas. This was approximately two miles from the ranch in Burnett, Texas. Despite the fact that my family did not attend church often at home, I enjoyed going to church. During a service in church one day. The preacher was Dr. Marshall Edwards from the Southern Baptist Convention. I remember a very quiet whisper deep down in my spirit saying "I want you to be a minister." At the time, I didn't realize it, but now I know that was God's voice. That was the first time I ever heard from God. I only know it was the voice of God because I've heard it on several occasions since then. I've never heard that voice steer me wrong. A peace that surpasses all understanding comes with that voice.

There was a boom like two one-thousand-watt subwoofers in the back seat of a Chevy truck. It was Dr. Marshall Edwards who said, "There is hope and victory in Jesus." The sermon was over and as we were heading back to the boys ranch that day. Since it was my first extended stay away from home in my lifetime, I remember missing home a great deal. The year would soon turn to 1991.

It took me a little less than two years to finish my time on the ranch before my family forced me to return home since my time there had come to an end and I voluntarily remained. I enjoyed my time there and was doing well. I returned home, met a girl, and began sexual activity with her immediately. Our first child was born three years later. When I was seventeen years old, I was already a father, and I had all the makings of an alcoholic in the near future. Once I reached the age of 18, I began chasing hailstorms in various parts of the Midwest. It did not take me long to begin making money hand over fist. The average annual income I would earn would be approximately $220,000. In some years, I would be able to earn approximately $350,000. A mere four years earlier, I had struggled for survival and watched my friends die from drug overdoses and murders in the ghetto. I was one of eight children living in poverty, eating out of trash cans a decade earlier.

MONEY DOESN'T SOLVE PROBLEMS

There is no denying that life is full of challenges. The problem with making all that money was that I was irresponsible. It was my addiction to strippers and to alcohol which led to me becoming an alcoholic. It is important to note that both of these addictions feed one another. There was a great deal of pride, ego, and fear within me. I experienced more addictions in the early millennium than a

115

cat has lives, and that number was nowhere near nine. I was addicted to everything the world had to offer, primarily money. It was truly an addiction of the highest order.

I worked from six in the morning until nine at night, selling roofing and making a great deal of money. Then I would call the strip club manager that I kept on speed dial and ask him to meet me at my condo and they would provide me with a limousine or Rolls Royce to get there at any time. At times, I would rent the limo myself for two thousand four hundred dollars a night, plus twenty percent gratuity, and I would still leave an additional four or five hundred dollars for the driver. As a young man of nineteen, I was the life of the party when I would attend clubs. It was not uncommon for me to spend thousands of dollars a night partying. During one night at Tiger's Gentleman's Club in Dallas, Texas, I spent almost $6,000. It is true that I had ninety-nine problems, but financial problems were not one of them. It was because I was capable of making a large amount of money quickly.

When I left the ghetto in Arlington, Texas, I made a promise to myself that I would never be poor. It was very difficult for me to go to bed hungry as a child. I was horrified to see my mother go hungry so that her children could eat. It was that fear of poverty that drove me to the brink of madness. It was the worst thought process I have ever experienced. I was driven to harm everyone and everything around me as a result of this. The experience was absolutely horrendous. I consider the money to be one of the worst things that has ever happened to me. My life would have been better off if I lived in the ghetto, poor and broke.

It was then that I began to ascend my way to the top of the residential roofing industry. In order to be the best I could be at what I did, I set out to eat, sleep, and breathe excellence. As far as my business life was concerned, it was impeccable. When it came to bidding insurance jobs, I was like a brain surgeon, and my clients regarded me as a true professional.

In a moment's notice, I could be ready to deploy a sales team and within forty-eight hours of being on the ground where the disaster struck. I was also able to dissect the storm, devise a strategy for optimizing sales in that area, and eliminating the competition, or at least minimizing it. In some ways, it was as if I had been born to sell roofing. It is with humility that I make this statement. I was one of the best in the business from 1998 to 2007. Since our sales teams made the contractors millions of dollars, the contractors loved me and my business partner to death. The experience was extraordinary!

At one point I was carrying around one hundred and twenty thousand cash on me with five bank accounts. As for change, I used to pick up change off the ground when I was a kid and ask people for change so I could buy a piece of candy. In my world, a twenty-dollar bill became change. It was crazy, I had a wife, children, and sadly was still acting like a child myself. I was like a kid in a candy store with all the money I needed to buy anything I wanted. It was terrible looking back now.

I would have the owner call me in the early morning hours, because he would fly in from the corporate office in Greenwood, Indiana. He would use a small plane that he flew around the Midwest in, after me and my partner made him a multimillionaire. I was laying there one time, and had just got to sleep and it was about four in the morning. My phone rang, and I'm laying there with this girl. I answered my phone, oops, wrong phone. The other one is still ringing. I answer it and the owner of the company says "I just flew in on my private plane, meet me at the airport. A monster hailstorm just pounded Columbus, Ohio." I woke up three hours later and made the flight from Minneapolis, Minnesota to Columbus, Ohio.

That was my life from eighteen to twenty-nine years old. It was one big party, chasing hailstorms, hurricanes, money, and strippers! The sad part about it is that although I made over two million and two hundred thousand dollars in about ten years. I really never enjoyed it. The money was cursed. A fool and his money soon parted! I was very foolish and I spent every bit of the money as fast as I made it. I did that with the thought process of "what is money made for? To spend right."

It was always my intention to live above my means and at any cost. I woke up every morning and lived every moment of my life for the sole purpose of making money. The people, the contractors, the clients, and the strippers were not of any concern to me. There were only three things I cared about: me, my money, and getting what I wanted from God's creation. It was my daily mantra that money would solve all my problems one by one, and I would expect more of it every day. All of this, while I stood by and watched my wives and children be exposed to such a horrific situation. The entire time, I was living in denial of what I was really searching for as I went about my daily life.

FALSE COMFORTERS AREN'T COMFORTERS

When it came to replacing the love of God in Christ Jesus, I had tried everything I could think of. Throughout my life, I've tried just about every false comforter the world had to offer to change how I felt on the inside, in order to be able to cope with my emotional state. It is sad to think that my wife and children had to stand by and watch me go down in a blaze of glory, despite the fact that they loved me dearly. My life was engulfed in a web of lies and deception. I was crowned with the riches of the world by the oldest slickster in the world, Satan himself. This was to distract me from what really matters in life and that is a relationship with God and His creation. I plunged head first into a sea of money and women, and I also fell into the abyss head first.

My personal life was beginning to go downhill and then the day arrived when my wife divorced me and I lost all hope. The second marriage I had would also fall apart, and I would be divorced again. I then went on to have a third marriage and my age was thirty-four, so as fate would have it, this third marriage ended in a divorce. First and foremost, I was stripped of my relationships with my wife and children, and that was the first thing I lost.

FALSE REALITY

In spite of this, I did not realize what was happening because I did not feel that I was a part of the problem that was causing it to happen. There was only one problem, and that was everyone else. That is what I kept telling myself over and over again in my head as I tried to overcome the feelings of fear. It was again a matter of working hard and playing harder as I went forward. As a result, the only thing I was doing was creating a false reality for myself, perhaps without even realizing that I was doing it. It's certainly possible that I was subconsciously doing it, but I don't know for sure. I am fully aware of the fact that this was a false reality I created and I have no doubts about that at all. It could be said that I lived a lie, or in other words, I was deceiving myself.

I used to go to strip clubs for women on a regular basis, no doubt about it. However, I also went because I found it a distraction from the real world, though not entirely true. I remember it being dark, there were no clocks on the walls, inexplicably, there were a lot of naked women running around, and at that moment, nothing mattered to me at all. It made me feel loved, needed, and wanted. At the time and place I was all that mattered. It was a desperate situation, and I was in dire need of help. As much as I tried to admit that I had a problem with alcohol, I could not do it. There was a sense of pride in me that I could not overcome. It would have been easier for me to die than to admit back then that I was an alcoholic. As a result, I kept going to work and generating income for myself.

HANGING BY A TETHER

It was only a matter of time until I began getting arrested for bar fights and domestic violence. As I was rapidly fading into the darkness, I began to lose sight of myself. There was a similarity between me and a comet streaking across the night sky. My rope was at the end of its length and I was at the end of my tether. The business partners I had been working with were stripped away from me, and I began to lose money as a result. I think it is also fair to say that my money was being stripped from me, as well. When I was in my second marriage, I was stripped of my condominium that was one block away from Ridglea Country Club, which is located in Fort Worth, Texas. I walked away with my clothes, my truck, and a certain amount of cash that I had hidden that nobody knew I had that was somewhere between seventy-five and eighty thousand dollars. There was a gradual rise in the amount of times I was getting arrested for driving while intoxicated and assaults. In terms of my physical freedom, you could definitely say that I was being stripped of it for certain. I started going down quick, fast, and in a hurry.

In a sense, the king and his crown are falling to the ground, so to speak. As I look back now, I can see that I was in a lot of circumstances that I would not have been in if I knew what I'm telling you now. There was a time a while ago when I could have clothed myself in humility and received God's grace. It is possible that I could have saved myself and a lot of other people from a great deal of heartache had I done that. As fate would have it, it wasn't to be. It was out of foolish pride that I continued to exalt myself above measure. As it says in the Bible, "For those who exalt themselves will be humbled, and those who humble themselves will be exalted" (Matthew 23:12, NIV, 2010). In my life, it seemed that the good Lord kept allowing me to lose everything I had. After all was said and done, I was stripped down to nothing but life itself. As a direct result of my actions, I was stripped of my home, cars, trucks, money, job, pride, ego, attitude, wives, children, friends, and family; I was stripped of everything that I owned.

IT'S ALL PERCEPTION

The reason for all of this was far more mysterious to me than the obvious reason that I believed there was. The obvious reason is because of the actions I have taken in the past. My belief is that the Lord, who is rich in mercy, has allowed me to be locked up all these years so that I would not die. The good Lord spared my life so

I could help you and others. It is my firm belief that if I had not spent those years in prison, I would have fought to the bitter end and died in my sin problem. The result of this is what occurs when a sin problem is left unattended by Jesus Christ. Interestingly, I blamed God for a long time for how my life turned out. The truth is that I now understand things differently.

In the Bible it says, "A person's own folly leads to their ruin, yet their heart rages against the Lord" (Proverbs 19:3, NIV, 2010). In my former life, I was similar to those people who blamed their life's circumstances on God. I cannot tell you how many times I have heard people do so, and they set themselves up as though they were a god, a position that they acquired through pride and ignorance of God's infallible Word. In the event that they failed, they attributed it to God. In the event that they were successful, they failed to give God credit for their accomplishments. There is no denying the horrific nature of pride. I know this to be true by experience.

The lesson I have learned is what they did not understand. It is our choice to be ignorant of the Word of God, and this keeps us living in defeat and mediocrity. It follows that the sin problem left unresolved by Jesus will result in physical death, and if you are fortunate enough to live, tomorrow is not guaranteed to anyone. This means that you lose twice without Jesus as your savior. The moment you die physically without Jesus as your savior, your eternal destiny is sealed. Our lives are not enriched when we do not develop a relationship with God and refrain from renewing our minds through the Word of God. The state of our existence is the same as that of a dead man. The only difference between a person in the grave and an unbeliever is that the former still has hope of repentance.

There is one thing I wish to assure you. It is impossible for you and I to reach our full potential without a personal relationship with God through Jesus Christ. Our existence is similar to a seed on a shelf. In other words, if the seed is not planted and the germination process is not triggered. There is no possibility of it reaching its full potential. The difference between an apple seed and an apple tree is significant. When an apple seed is planted and germination begins, it becomes an apple tree as it matures. It is the same way when we are unbelievers. We can never begin to recognize our potential without salvation and transformation. Jesus replied, "Very truly I tell you, no one can see the kingdom of God unless they are born again" (John 3:3, NIV, 2010).

SEEKING SOMETHING BEYOND THIS WORLD

It is possible to live an awesome life without Jesus and still be successful. Take a look at the world's richest men and women. The thing that you are really searching for, my friend, cannot be found in this world. What you really want is to fill the void in your heart, and that God-shaped void acts as an internal compass that guides you to Him. It is God's love that fills that void. The purpose of this is to enable you to receive the grace of God through the way of humility and Jesus Christ. This will lead to the attainment of true life, eternal life, abundant life, joy, peace, contentment, and a sense of purpose.

Moreover, you will also have a new heart, because you will be a new creation, and everything that you say, think, or do will be motivated by love for God, because He is worthy! This is what Jesus does when a person accepts him as their Savior. My statement is not based on information that I have heard. My story is based on a spiritual experience that I have had. I don't know who you are. I have no idea what you have been through. There is no doubt in my mind that God does. It is true that I experienced a living hell for twenty-nine years and almost died at forty-one years of age as a result of my ignorance.

As I lay in my cell that day at the Hancock County Jail, it was as if I had already died. It was as if I had disappeared. My identity in Christ had been robbed by the enemy of our souls, and I was a willing accomplice because I chose to be ignorant of the Word of

God, thus leading me automatically to live a lie. I was fortunate in that God is rich in mercy. My life at the age of forty-one was coming to an end as I lay there. My life had become completely hopeless and despairing after I had learned this. He shocked me into a greater awareness of his amazing grace, through the way of humility, and Jesus Christ.

WORTHY OF BEING LOVED

All of my life I was similar to the older brother in the parable of the prodigal son in Luke 15. This story of the prodigal son illustrates how the older brother represents our rational resistance to God's forgiveness. The way I had been my entire life was exactly the same. I believed that God would only love me if I was good enough. In spite of being a good man, my earthly father was incapable of properly giving and receiving love. Throughout my life, I heard three times from my father that he loved me and I believed that I was not good enough for God or anyone else to love me. The result was that my thought process ultimately led me down a path of self-destruction and almost cost me my life. I lay there in all my helplessness that day, withdrawing from heroin in that cell at the Hancock County Jail. My life had never been so dark as when I was in that place. There appeared to be no hope left. There is, however, a God of restoration!

GOD'S UNCONDITIONAL LOVE

While lying in the cell that day, the sight of my mother putting me on the church bus when I was five years old reminded me that there was hope, because God is a living hope, a hope that is unconditional. I am grateful to God for sending his son to die for me while I was a sinner. He did this when I was not good enough, and that was why I needed his grace. I needed to feel that my Heavenly Father loved, needed, and wanted me.

The experience was like God had not only humbled me through my circumstances, but also shocked me into an awareness of his amazing grace. The concept of grace, by definition, refers to something that cannot be earned or deserved. I then reached out to God in all my helplessness and said "God please let me die." After having been stripped of everything in life and nearly life itself, I wished for death. The good news is that God, who is so rich in love, grace, and mercy, reached down to answer my prayer, but it was not in the way I envisioned it, not in my wildest dreams.

Then, God proceeded to show me I would need to do what Jesus said "If anyone came after me, he must give up his own life, take up his cross, and follow me daily." (Luke 9:23, NIV, 2010). "Those who try to save their life, will lose it. But those who lose their lives for my name's sake and the gospels sake will save it" (Luke 9:24, NIV, 2010). I lived for forty-one years in a self-imposed prison of pride. I thank God that I was able to accept God's grace.

After allowing me to be stripped of everything so that I could see that I needed to receive his love, grace and mercy, the good Lord had finally managed to get me to my eternal home through the way of humility, Jesus Christ. It is through his gift of mercy that the Lord Jesus Christ has provided for us. I want to leave you with one verse from the Bible. I learned very early on in my Christian walk that I needed to learn how to die, if I was going to learn how to live. The Bible says, "For to me, to live is Christ and to die is gain" (Philippians 1:21, NIV, 2010). There is no greater need in the world than Jesus Christ. As a result of His teachings, I learned how to die to myself, so that I could live for Him. Hence, to die is gain! It is my sincere hope that you will find what you are seeking in the love of God in Christ Jesus my friend. May God bless you and keep you safe for the remainder of your life. I pray that the grace of the Lord Jesus Christ, the son of the one and only true God, be with you at all times (Revelation 22:21, NIV, 2010).